I Believe in Revelation

by

LEON MORRIS

WILLIAM B. EERDMANS PUBLISHING COMPANY

First Printing, February 1976
Second Printing, June 1977

Library of Congress Cataloging in Publication Data

Morris, Leon, 1914-
    I believe in revelation.

    Includes bibliographical references.
    1. Revelation.   I. Title.
BT127.2.M64 1976   231'.74   75-45349
ISBN 0-8028-1637-1

I Believe in Revelation

Contents

Editor's Preface

It all started at lunch, appropriately enough at a meeting of the Church of England's Doctrine Commission. I had been chatting about this forthcoming series with Dr. G. W. H. Lampe, Regius Professor of Divinity at Cambridge. He said, "I hope you are including one on 'I Believe in Revelation' ". I am not sure that we were at that stage, but thereafter it seemed inevitable. Because, unfashionable though the subject of revelation is these days, it still remains the ultimate question underlying so many of the more obviously contemporary issues.

Thus comparative religion is an exceedingly fashionable matter in educational circles today, with the assumption that all religions are much of a muchness, and all record man's striving towards God. But what if it is not possible for man in his search to arrive at God, and God has instead shown himself to man? That is a big 'if', to be sure. But *if* that is the case, then all religions are not much of a muchness. In one (or possibly more) of them God may have spoken. It is vital to see if he has.

Another pressing modern concern is what Sir Alister Hardy has attempted in his *The Biology of God*, the recovery of a credible natural theology. Has God, or has he not, disclosed himself in the way his world works? Are there moral as well as physical laws which govern its well being? This is a most pressing problem, because of the ever increasing advance in scientific knowledge and the awesome moral responsibilities some of the discoveries bring with them.

Again, while it is true that there is currently considerable thirst for some kind of religious experience, it is often allied to profound scepticism not merely about Christianity but about absolute truth of any kind. This brings us sharply back to the question of revelation: is there any place where truth and experience coincide? Is there any religious experience which is not merely 'their thing' for those who engage in it, but brings them into touch with what is ultimately real?

These are general questions in our society which come back to the issue of revelation in the last instance. And in theological circles the matter is no less cardinal. For it is one of the basic assumptions of the modern critical method that the Bible is in all respects to be treated exactly like any other ancient book. But if (and only if) God has disclosed himself in and through the pages of the Bible, then it cannot be adequate to treat it as precisely on a par with all the rest.

This 'if' is the cardinal issue which Dr. Morris has set himself to examine in the pages that follow. Can we, or can we no longer, speak meaningfully of God's self-revelation in nature and in Scripture? He is well known throughout the world as a prolific writer, a careful and reverent New Testament scholar and a man who has a high regard for the trustworthiness of the Bible. He had never written a book on this subject, though he had handled it often enough in a variety of ways, and I was delighted that he was able to accept with enthusiasm my invitation to contribute this very important volume to the series. I hope it will be widely read, not least by those about to embark on academic theology. And I am sure that nobody will read it without great profit.

Michael Green

CHAPTER I

The Place of Revelation

"*The Old Testament writers do not pretend that the relation of God and Man is close enough or clear enough for God to be said to have revealed himself.*" The New Testament writers "never clearly and explicitly say that 'God reveals himself (in Christ)', of that 'God has revealed himself'." In words like these F. Gerald Downing makes it plain that he rejects traditional ideas of revelation. And he is far from being alone. James Barr has written in highly critical terms of generally accepted ideas of revelation while Christopher Evans can entitle a book *Is "Holy Scripture" Christian?* And there are others.

In the face of a widespread denial of the reality or the relevance of revelation it is plain that Christians today must do some hard thinking. We can no longer take revelation for granted. Should we reject the whole traditional idea of revelation? Or the ways in which it has been formulated? If so, what do we put in its place? If not, what are we to say of the very forceful criticisms that are being put forward? Such questions cannot simply be glossed over.

What is Revelation?

Let us begin on the level of definition. We must be clear on what we understand by the term. According to *The Shorter Oxford English Dictionary* revelation means in the first place, "The disclosure of knowledge to man by a divine or supernatural agency", and secondly, "Something disclosed or made known by divine or supernatural means". Theologians might hesitate over this concentration on knowledge, for some of them would certainly prefer to define revelation in terms of the disclosure of a person. But the point on which we fasten our attention is the

word "disclosure". Revelation is not concerned with knowledge
we once had but have forgotten for the time being. Nor does it
refer to the kind of knowledge that we might attain by diligent
research. It is knowledge that comes to us from outside ourselves and beyond our own ability to discover.

It is knowledge that someone else discloses to us. In
Christianity the term is important for it means that God has
taken the initiative in disclosing himself to man. The knowledge
of God is thought of then not as the end product of diligent
human search, but as a manifestation of God's grace and of his
will to be known.

Traditionally Christians have been firm believers in revelation. To take an example at random, Dr. Sigfrid Estborn can
say simply, "We Christians believe that Jesus Christ is the Son
of God, that he has revealed God to us. . . ."[2] He does not argue.
He assumes the point. He takes revelation to be fundamental.
And his is no exceptional position. To most Christians it is
axiomatic. It simply states the obvious. In the opening chapter
of their Bible they are confronted with a God who speaks and
they find him speaking throughout their Bible. The God of the
Bible is a God who speaks to man.

Believers have varied somewhat in the way they understand
this revelation and in the extent to which they see it operating.
Some have taken the whole Bible from cover to cover as the
word of God, divinely inspired and to be accepted without
question. For them everything in the Bible is revelation. Others
have felt that God has given us the treasure in earthen vessels
and they have sometimes seen these vessels as pretty fallible.
So they have thought of men as inspired to write down important truths but as mingling with the eternal the temporal
and the fallacious. Prophets, lawgivers, evangelists and the rest
have written out of their own cultural situation and in the
process have given expression to their own physical, mental and
spiritual limitations. They have thus given us a full measure of
their insights, but also a full measure of their own personal
errors and of the errors of their day. People who see the Bible in
this light have exercised care in sifting the true from the false.
But when they have finished they have held that the residue of
truth that is left represents what God has revealed to man and
not what godly men of old have reasoned out for themselves.
The very great differences in the ways men have understood
both the manner and the extent of revelation serves to high-
light their impressive agreement on the fact of revelation.

Again, some have insisted that the revelation is propositional. They hold that what God revealed is given in words ("verbal inspiration"). They see no great meaning in a revelation in ideas which must then be shaped by men as best they can. So they emphasise the precise words that have come down to us. Others dismiss this view in favour of the idea that God inspired men rather than words. They think of the prophets, for example, as men aglow with the divine Spirit. They are not greatly interested in the precise words in which the prophets expressed their message, but they are convinced that they did have a message to express. Sometimes this is understood in the sense that what is revealed is God, not any proposition about God. The inspired authors are then men who have come into vital contact with God and who, as a result, have something to say that they think men must heed. The revelation of God is real. There is a divine disclosure. But the manner in which it is expressed belongs to the writer and not to the revelation. Others again see the revelation as both propositional and personal. They think that God has revealed himself, but that he has also revealed truth about himself.

There are thus some not unimportant differences in the way Christians have understood revelation. But common to these divergent views is the thought that God has disclosed himself. There are differences as to whether he has done this in a series of propositions, whether he has disclosed himself directly, or whether he has done both. But none of the approaches we have been considering sees men as left unaided when they seek to discover truth about God and man and the relationship between them. They all take revelation seriously. Indeed, for the most part they regard revealed truth as the very foundation of all Christian understanding whether of this world or that to come. Christians are seen as men who think and live on the basis of what God has done for them and made known to them.

It is this revelation of God which has always been seen as basic to serious study of theology. Man as man has no access to the inner life of God, no knowledge of God's essential being. Theology is not a study of "God-in-himself" but of "God-as-he-has-revealed-himself". The theologian, it has been held, must always do his work on the basis of what has been revealed. He has no access to the inner life of God, no knowledge of what God is in himself. The theologian has been prepared to go along with the scriptural emphasis that God reveals himself. The Old Testament is insistent that God is a God who speaks. Indeed, for the Old Testament writers this is a principal difference from the heathen gods who are nothing but dumb idols: "They have mouths, but do not speak . . . they do not make a sound in their throat" (Ps. 115: 5, 7). By contrast, "I the Lord will speak the word which I will speak" (Ezek. 12: 25). It is not otherwise in the New Testament. The same God who spoke of old has now spoken in his Son (Heb. 1 : 1f.). Indeed, a New Testament writer refers to "him who speaks" (Heb. 12 : 25). God spoke to Paul (Acts 18: 9). Throughout the Bible the term "God" is used of One who has revealed himself. It does not refer to a deity thought up by man.

Denial of Revelation
The modern denial of revelation develops from the idea that the words in which the revelation is expressed are of no great importance. God has given the context of the message but allowed men to give it shape in their own way and in their own words. Some of those words are taken to be erroneous, partly as a result of the limitations of the messengers and partly because of the limitations of the societies in which they lived and which gave them so many of their ideas and their ways of expressing ideas. Once granted that there is error it is possible to go far and go fast. This is, of course, not inevitable, and some who see error in the Bible see also God's revealed truth. But others reason that we may, indeed we must discard many statements of the biblical authors. And if words may be rejected so, of course, may ideas. Carry this process far enough and we are left with nothing more than the thoughts of men of bygone ages.

It may then not unreasonably be asked, "Why should we, with all our advances over men of early days in so many areas of life, give any special place to these ancient writings?" Radical opinion, as James Barr points out, is apt to ask, "*Why the Bible*? Why should a group of ancient books have this dominant status? If a group of ancient books, then why *this* group of ancient books? And why in any case should anyone suppose that any objective external authority, in the shape of a group of books or any other shape at all, exists at all?"[3]

Those who reason like this have rejected revelation in any meaningful sense, whatever nods they may make to orthodoxy. Scripture is for them no longer the supremely normative book. In fact it is straining language to speak of it as normative at all.

This development means a critical attitude towards the whole Bible including the words of Jesus. Many New Testament scholars have been hesitant about the extent to which we should accept as authentic the teaching ascribed to Jesus in the Gospels. But in the end they have usually found some teaching which they feel may confidently be ascribed to the Master. Up till recently it has been thought that all Christians would take such sayings as fully authoritative. They come from the incarnate Son of God and they must therefore be accepted and obeyed by these who follow that Son of God.

But the recent approach will not allow even this. Jesus, after all, was a first-century man. Like all other men of his day he accepted the unquestioned errors of his time. We should pay due respect to what he says, but not regard his words as final and authoritative. Since in addition there are errors in reporting, the conclusion is reached that we need not be over-impressed by the Gospels. Even when we can recover the words of Jesus they are no more than the words of a first-century religious teacher. A. O. Dyson, for example, refers to the view that "God has vouchsafed to us in Jesus Christ a revelation", but he sees this as no more than a theory. Moreover it is a theory with a problem "as to what constitutes this revelation". Having reduced revelation to the status of a questionable theory, he can say things like, "If the revelation theory cannot be used . . .", "I take the view that we cannot in fact *begin* our enquiry about Jesus Christ from a supposed revelation."[4]

Dyson cites other recent writers who are exercised about the concept of revelation and he goes on to suggest that the concept itself is no more than a comparatively recent development. He thinks its date unimportant but he is inclined to say "that the great breach in the dam took place only in the seventeenth and eighteenth centuries". He cites Gerhard Ebeling for the view that in modern times Christianity has lost "the self-evident validity" it had had in the Western world for more than a millennium.[5]

> Thus the history of Christian theology in the last three centuries may, for the greater part, be not unfairly described as a series of retreating retaliations to that crisis. . . . It is within this overall process that the notion of revelation has been introduced as a device by which a stable foundation may be supplied for Christian thought and life.[6]

Dyson rejects such an introduction of revelation.

A New Religion?

If this is the way of it then Christianity has been transformed. God may not be dead but traditional Christianity certainly is and the question arises, "Are we not confronted by a new religion?" Instead of basing our beliefs on what God has made known we are now asked to base them on our own best insights. We may take some notice of the classical exponents of Christianity, but in the last resort what we accept is nothing more than the ideas that happen to commend themselves to us personally. It is also the case that if we are to take notice of the classical exponents of Christianity simply as men who give us useful ideas to consider we may as well do the same with thinkers outside the Bible as those inside it. It would be impossible to deny that many thinkers outside Christianity have·given us ideas on which we may profitably reflect and act. There is as much (or as little) authority in such thinkers as in the writers of the books of the Bible. This approach effectively does away with the Bible as the deposit of revealed truth.

For this reason it is important to take a fresh look at the concept of revelation. Have Christians been wrong about this for nineteen hundred years? Should we now give up the idea of studying the Bible, other than in the sense in which we study the writings of say, Cyprian? Should we have the courage of our convictions and cease to read the Bible in our services of worship? Should we stop giving it pride of place in our private devotions? Questions multiply and they cannot be shrugged off as unimportant. It is one thing to make constant reference to a book one regards as authoritative. It is quite another to form one's ideas irrespective of what some ancient scrolls have to say. And this question must be decided at the outset. Until we know the answer we are going to give to it we cannot well face anything else. We must know where the basis for our theology is to be found.

The problem affects all Christians and all churches and it affects also the relationships that Christians and churches have with one another. We have often assumed happily that since all Christians have the Bible in common there is at least a common basis on which we may begin our discussions across the denominations. But unless we agree on the way the Bible is to be used and the extent to which it is authoritative there is no more than a façade of unity. This makes some resolution of the question important, or so it seems.

James Barr does not appear to think so, however. He

notices that "the status and value of the Bible is very much in question" and goes on to say, "such a situation may well come to be permanent".[7] This seems to mean that the Bible will be a subject for continuing discussion with no consensus in sight. That is to say, there will be no agreed and accepted authority. Some will value the Bible highly and others will practically disregard it, with neither apparently being any more right than the other. Each man will be his own authority. We are shut up to a subjectivity that is poles apart from the traditional appeal to an authoritative word from God.

Barr holds that for many the issue will be something like this: "are theology and doctrine (and thereby preaching also) based upon something that we have received, that has been given to us; or do they in the last resort depend upon and consist of no more than our own ideas, however philosophically refined?"[8] On the face of it this is a serious divergence. But Barr apparently does not think that in the last resort our own ideas and those of the Bible are so very different: "we must judge that biblical ideas can and do very easily become 'our own ideas', and that this is just what happens with zealous biblicistic people."[9]

It is, of course, the case that people take over ideas from the Bible and make them their own. It is also, alas, the case that people all too readily take their own ideas and read them back into the Bible. But the point is not so easily disposed of. It is still a fact that there are ideas in the Bible that are not "our own ideas" and that when we go to the Bible humbly and in a spirit of readiness to learn we find them there. It is not necessary to argue ourselves into a position where we must hold that nobody can learn from the Bible. Many can and do. All Bible study cannot be reduced to an exercise in subjectivity. It is not necessary either to read back our own ideas into the Bible. It is possible to sit humbly before the Bible and let it speak to us. Granted that nobody can read the Bible without presuppositions it is still true that honest students make allowance for these presuppositions. Scholarly exegesis would be impossible otherwise. But throughout the world biblical scholars are constantly at work on exegetical labours, confident that they can say things that will make sense to their colleagues.

It is what the Bible says and not what Christians bring to it that is authoritative. This means that we cannot allow the divergence of which Barr speaks to determine the issue. It is true that divergent approaches are to be found. It may also be the case that these approaches will be with us for a long time to come, as Barr thinks. But even if so, this does not dispose of the question. We cannot on that basis say, "Since there are going to be different opinions the whole matter of revelation is settled." The possibility arises that one or other of these opinions may be wrong. What Barr has to say serves as a warning that the issues are complex, so complex that in the end people may still differ. But this does not excuse us from a serious examination of the question, "Has God spoken?" If he has, we go our subjective way at our peril.

A similar comment might be made about other approaches which have a tendency to bypass the question of revelation. Some students of the Bible and of Christianity tend to concentrate on questions about relevance and in the process find sections of the Bible of little use for they do not seem to impinge on our modern society. Others ask questions about the theory of communication and wonder how ideas pass from one to another and whether it is possible to pick up ideas from God. Again it is possible to concentrate on the limitations inherent in the written word and to ask how the biblical writers can pass on what they have learned. These and similar questions are all peripheral. They have their importance and they must be studied carefully. But none of them excuses us from going to the heart of the matter and asking whether God has in fact chosen to reveal himself.

Bible Teaching about Revelation

The general concept of revelation is not a subject for discussion in the Bible. There the interest is rather in specific acts of revelation. We can consider them and reflect on their implications for the wider concept. But the biblical writers do not give us a full-scale treatment of the subject.

Perhaps most significant for our purpose are those passages which speak in some way of the revelation of God. "No one knows the Father", Jesus is recorded as saying, "except the Son and any one to whom the Son chooses to reveal him" (Matt. 11:27; cf. Luke 10:22). Downing tries to turn the thrust of this passage by maintaining that if it comes from Jesus or the earliest church "there is no room in it for any 'revealing' of *God himself*. . . . If Jesus 'reveals' anything, it is the demand of God, the demand inherent in this being the end-time. He does not 'reveal' God."[10] But this seems arbitrary. It is certainly not what the text says. "Any one to whom the Son chooses to reveal him" is specific enough and it is concerned with the revelation of God not with any demands that God makes.

Sometimes it is the Son who is said to be revealed, as when Paul says that God "was pleased to reveal his Son to me" (Gal. 1 : 16), or when Jesus says, with reference to Peter's affirmation that he was the Christ, "flesh and blood has not revealed this to you, but my Father who is in heaven" (Matt. 16 : 17). Such passages indicate that the divine is not known to men. But they indicate also that the divine may be willing to disclose itself and that on occasion it has done so. Revelation is not within the control of men. They cannot demand it. But they can be given it in God's good time.

There are other passages in which a variety of divine qualities is said to have been revealed. This is true of God's glory (Isa. 40 : 5; cf. Rom. 8 : 18, 1 Pet. 4 : 13, 5 : 1), of the arm of the Lord (Isa. 53 : 1, John 12 : 38), the righteousness of God (Isa. 56 : 1, Rom. 1 : 17), his righteous judgment (Rom. 2 : 5), his wrath (Rom. 1 : 18) and more. These passages bring us into the same circle of ideas. They confront us with the thought that man of himself cannot know what God is and is like. Any knowledge of this kind must be disclosed to him.

Perhaps the most important passages under this heading are those which speak of the gospel as revealed. Paul says explicitly, "the gospel which was preached by me is not man's gospel. For I did not receive it from man, nor was I taught it, but it came through a revelation of Jesus Christ" (Gal. 1 : 11f.). He probably has much the same thought in mind when he speaks of "faith" as being revealed (Gal. 3 : 23). Sometimes the gospel is in mind when a "mystery" is said to be revealed, as in the closing section of Romans with its reference to "my gospel and the preaching of Jesus Christ, according to the revelation of the mystery which was kept secret for long ages but is now disclosed" (Rom. 16 : 25f.). The mystery may be connected with the place of the Gentiles in God's purposes (Eph. 3 : 3-6); it is still the gospel that is in view as we see from verse 7). That God included Gentile believers within the scope of his salvation is not seen as a truism. It is a startling disclosure, to be received with awe and thankfulness. Expressions like "the mystery of the faith" and "the mystery of our religion" (1 Tim. 3 : 9, 16) are affirmations that the essential teachings of Christianity are truths made known by revelation, not worked out by the unaided human mind.

The point of all this is apparently that no man would or

could ever have worked out the idea of the gospel (and of the place of the Gentiles in it) for himself. It seems so clear to the natural man that one's final destiny is determined by oneself that it needed revelation for him to realise that it depends rather on the grace of God. Revelation is needed, too, to know that the working out of that grace involved the incarnation, the life of Jesus of Nazareth, his atoning death, his resurrection and ascension. This is indeed "mystery". But it has now been made known.

So far it could be said that all fits in with the great principle laid down in Deuteronomy 29: 29: "The secret things belong to the Lord our God; but the things that are revealed belong to us and to our children for ever, that we may do all the words of this law." The revelation is meant not only for those who actually received it but for their descendants as well. It is for the practical purpose of giving them guidance about the important matter of daily living in the service of God. Revelation is significant and is concerned with great matters.

But an interesting group of passages uses the terms "reveal" and "revelation" about things which by comparison are very minor. Thus Paul can speak of the Corinthian Christians coming together for worship and say, "When you come together, each one has a hymn, a lesson, a revelation . . ." (1 Cor. 14: 26). This "revelation" seems no more than a helpful thought to be contributed to the Sunday worship service, albeit a thought that has come from God rather than man. Someone who is ready to speak at such a time of worship must remain silent instead "If a revelation is made to another sitting by" (1 Cor. 14: 30). It is probably this sort of thing that Paul has in mind when he speaks of bringing a revelation (1 Cor. 14: 6) or of the abundance of the revelations (2 Cor. 12: 1, 7). Here, too, we should understand the apostle's conviction that on one occasion he went up to Jerusalem "by revelation" (Gal. 2: 2), and perhaps also his view that if the Philippians required it God would give them a revelation (Phil. 3: 15).

Compared with the great truths of the faith perhaps these "revelations" may seem trivial. But they point to an important truth, namely that the Spirit of God does not leave his own. We are not to think of revelation as something once given in the sense that the Spirit henceforth withdraws and lets the people of God do the best they can with the definitive deposit. Rather, he is among them constantly. They can rely on a dynamic presence of God which continually supplies what they need.

Such in brief outline appears to be the principal teaching of the Bible on the express subject of revelation. It is not large in amount and some have drawn the conclusion that the whole concept of revelation is not important for the Bible writers. This, however, is too facile. If we wish to know what the writers of the Biblical books thought about revelation we must take into account a good deal more than the passages which contain the noun "revelation" of the verb "reveal". Thus Dewey M. Beegle discusses not only revelation, but also word, teaching, name, glory, prediction, wisdom, manifestation and path or way. He goes on to notice that other words also contain the idea of revelation as commandment, announcement, proclamation, promise, knowledge, counsel, truth, tradition, testimony, covenant, appearance and light. When he comes to consider verbs he lists reveal, prophesy, foretell, speak and know, and points out also the relevance of appear, lead (guide), open, shine, bear witness, promise and proclaim.[11] It is not possible for us to deal with this vast mass of evidence, but at least we should notice that it is there. It is not, of course, con- tended that every example of the use of every word in these lists is a further example of revelation. That is not so. But no one who knows his Bible can deny that all of them can be used on occasion to convey the idea of revelation and that some of them are usually used in this way.

Modern Doubts

It is important to notice this because it seems to be overlooked in the work of F. Gerald Downing to which we have already referred, *Has Christianity a Revelation?* He has drawn the fewness of the biblical references to revelation into an argument that the whole concept is foreign to Christianity. But it may be doubted whether he has really faced the teaching of the Bible on this subject. His method is heavily statistical and linguistic. He argues that the passages containing the various words for "reveal" and the like are few in number. He argues further that the meaning of "reveal" is to give clear and accurate knowledge. Indeed one of his principal arguments against the whole con- cept of revelation in Christianity is that Christians have drawn such divergent ideas from the Bible. If there really were revelation given by God then everyone would see it. The fact that all do not see it is evidence in itself that God has not given a revelation at all. Downing rejects the idea that God is a bungler who could give a revelation only in such a way that people could not understand what He was saying. Revelation means "making clear". What is not clear is not revelation and we are misusing our terms if we apply "revelation" to what people interpret as divergently as they do the Bible. Nor can we rescue ourselves by claiming that the revelation is "partial" or "gradual" or the like. In that case, Downing thinks, "The theologian is using a word that normally describes 'making clear' to mean 'leave unclear'. It is not very helpful."[12]

Downing has argued his case magnificently. It is not easy to fault him. But one reader at least does not find his blameless reasoning convincing. For the fact is that Downing never gets round to asking questions like, "Did the Bible writers claim to have real knowledge of God or did they not?" "If they did, did they work it out for themselves or did God disclose it?" It is eminently satisfying to the scholarly mind to work through the occurrences of, say, *galah* and come to the conclusion that it does not help us to see revelation in the Bible. But it is completely irrelevant to more important questions like: "Did Abraham really know God?", "Did Moses?", "Has what these men knew of God been recorded in such a way that it becomes available for other men?".

The trouble is that Downing is arguing in an *a priori* manner. To be sure, he disclaims this. He repudiates "deductive reasoning about the 'nature' of God" and holds that if someone suggests that "God" is "revealed" this is to be checked "not by wishful thinking, nor by its attractiveness, but by looking to the area of events to which this believer points".[13] But is this what in fact he has done? It seems not. For example, quite early in the piece he nominates three Hebrew words, *galah*, *'arah* and *hasap*, which have much the same meaning as the Greek *apokaluptein* and the Latin *revelare* and proceeds, "If any of the writers in the Old Testament used anything that might meaningfully be called 'a concept of revelation', it would seem fair to expect it to be expressed by one of these words."[14] In the same spirit of fairness he throws in other words, like *ra'ah* and *yada'* (both in the niphal) and examines them minutely. This enables him to draw the conclusion quoted in my opening sentence, that the Old Testament writers do not claim a sufficiently close relation between God and man for God to be said to have revealed himself.

But with all respect, that is surely not the way to approach the subject. Downing is saying in effect: "If the Old Testament writers want to convey the idea of revelation they must do it in the way I lay down. It is inconceivable that they should do it in a different way." But the question immediately arises, "Is it?" Downing's *a priori* assumption does not allow the Bible writers to choose their own way. They must do it Downing's way or they cannot do it at all.

Would it not be a better idea to ask what they have in fact done and let them speak for themselves? There seems no reason why a prophet should not be convinced that God is speaking through him, even though he never explicitly enunciates a concept of revelation. He may have no fancy notions of the way God communicates with men and thus never venture into speculations about how revelation takes place and yet be quite convinced that God is speaking through him. What else does "Thus saith the Lord" mean on the lips of a prophet? To take an example at random, it is not easy to think that, when Isaiah wrote "the Lord said to me" (Isa. 8: 1), he meant that he was about to give us a thought of his own. He is making no use of concepts like revelation. He is making no use of words like *galah*, *'arah* or *ḥaśap* (or even the niphal of *ra'ah* or *yada'*). But he is claiming that what follows is God's command to him. And that means revelation, whether the prophet chooses to use the term or not.

This could be said over and over again. Take this opening to an oracle of Jeremiah's: "The word that came to Jeremiah from the Lord: 'Stand in the gate of the Lord's house, and proclaim there this word, and say, Hear the word of the Lord. . . . Thus says the Lord of hosts . . .' " (Jer. 7: 1-3). Or Ezekiel's report of his vision of "the appearance of the likeness of the glory of the Lord." He says, "when I saw it, I fell upon my face, and I heard the voice of one speaking" (Ezek. 1: 28). I cannot see why men should write in this way if what they wanted to tell us was that they had given the matter thought and were now prepared to let us have their considered conclusions. If words mean anything they are reporting disclosures. They are saying that God spoke to them, revealed himself to them if you like.

All this must be taken with the utmost seriousness. My quarrel with Downing is not that he has not taken sufficient care along the lines of his investigation. On the contrary, I am full of admiration for the excellent and painstaking work he has done. He has drawn our attention to some interesting statistics and warned us against taking traditional positions for granted. It is hard to see what more should be done along that road. My quarrel with him is that he seems to me to be on the wrong road altogether. He will not let the biblical authors speak for themselves. He demands that they use his categories. This *a priori* approach seems all wrong.

When we let the Bible writers speak for themselves and simply listen to what they are saying we find them insisting very strongly that they are recording what God has said to them. They are not claiming to give us their own best thoughts on the topics of the day. They may not use our term but they are recording what we call revelation. Earlier we noticed A. O. Dyson's rejection of the concept of revelation. He espouses an open approach and holds that "we must above all be attentive to evidence".[15]

With this I am in full agreement. Indeed my complaint is that Dyson has given too little attention to this requirement. In some areas, it is true, he is scrupulous in attending to the evidence. He listens carefully to what historical criticism has to say. But not to the evidence for revelation. He never gets round to asking what the Bible says about itself and about revelation. He never looks at the evidence that the Bible writers held themselves to be conveying the very word of God nor asks why they should make such claims.

Yet these are the really important questions. The case for regarding Christianity as a religion of revelation does not rest on some changes in thought which Dyson or someone else postulates for the seventeenth or eighteenth centuries. It rests on the teaching of Christ and his apostles. If we are claiming to be "Christian" I cannot see any substitute for beginning with what the Christ taught. If that agrees with historical criticism or with modern liberalism or conservatism or fundamentalism or what you will so much the better for the favoured group. But, let the chips fall where they will, I see no substitute for beginning here.

A further defect in Dyson's approach is that it gives the decisive voice to the modern world. I do not see how we who live in that world can do anything other than pay respect to the ideas of our day. After all, they are the ideas of the community that we help to form. But it is quite another thing to give the voice of that community the determining voice. This is a day of great technology and science. But it is not a day of great art or great literature or great philosophy. There seems no reason for affirming that in religion our day is so great that it can decide crucial questions out of its own resources. Yet

THE PLACE OF REVELATION

Dyson can say, "At the end of the day, however, we have to affirm that, because the tradition about Jesus Christ is mediated (as much in the New Testament as anywhere else) through understandings of the world, those understandings of the world will call the tune in mobilising, sifting and appropriating that tradition."[16]

This is quite clear. But if the "understandings of the world" are going to "call the tune" then revelation is not given a chance. Anywhere a difficulty arises then by definition it is "the world" and not the Bible that counts. Revelation is excluded. I do not think that this approach is either fair or Christian. It is not fair because the revelation is not allowed to speak for itself. And it is not Christian, for it is the Christian attitude to give priority to Christ, not the world.

Men who Heard God

When we turn to the Bible there is good evidence that it is the voice of God which is decisive, not the best thoughts of saintly men of old. There are some very instructive passages in the prophecy of Jeremiah. Take, for example, that in which the prophet tells us that the Lord instructed him to exercise his right of redemption to the field of Hanamel, his uncle Shallum's son (Jer. 32). This made no sense to Jeremiah. Under what he took to be divine direction he had been prophesying consistently that the Babylonians would succeed in their attack on Jerusalem. When this prophecy was fulfilled Israelite rights to land would not matter in the slightest. What good would owning property back in Judea do a man in exile in Babylon? But the command to buy the field came from God (Jer. 32 : 6-8). So, though it made no sense to him, Jeremiah bought the field. And he did it properly. He paid the due price, seventeen shekels, and he had the deed properly signed, sealed, witnessed and deposited. He complied faithfully with all the legal requirements.

If that were all we might perhaps reason that Jeremiah was acting under some inner compulsion which he described as a command of God but which was really his own idea. The ascription to God was a rationalisation.

But Jeremiah goes on to a prayer of expostulation. He is perplexed. He cannot understand what God is telling him to do. God seems to be contradicting himself and Jeremiah does not like it one little bit. So he prays complaining. He begins by reminding God of his constant love to his people, of his power

and of the way he has worked in the history of the nation. But
Israel had proved faithless and God had sent the Babylonians
against her as a result. Jeremiah says to God,

> they would do nothing you ordered them to do; and so you
> made all these disasters happen to them. See how the earth-
> works grow nearer to the city for the assault! Sword, famine,
> and plague will deliver the city into the hands of the attack-
> ing Chaldaeans. What you have said is now fulfilled, as you
> see. Yet you yourself, Lord Yahweh, told me, "Buy the field
> with money in front of witnesses"—and even now the city is
> falling into the hands of the Chaldaeans! (Jer. 32 : 23-25,
> Jerusalem Bible).

Clearly this "word of the Lord" was not something that
Jeremiah himself had dreamed up from his own best insights.
When it came he could obey it. But he did not pretend to
understand it. After God had told him that the people would be
given into the hands of the Babylonians he could not see why
God should tell him to buy land. That made no sense to
Jeremiah. It was not as though the Babylonian threat was
remote and might possibly be averted. Hostile armies were at
that very moment investing the city. "You can see it yourself,
God" is a nice touch in the prophet's prayer. He does not tell
us how he could recognise the word of God when it came but
clearly it was something objective. For Jeremiah it was certain
that God spoke and that sometimes he spoke in ways that his
servant not only did not understand but objected to. But it does
not seem to have occurred to him that that gave the servant
the right to deny the divine origin of the message.

Jeremiah's conviction that Judah would return to its own
land after a period in captivity is clear. Elsewhere he even put a
time limit of seventy years on the duration of the exile (Jer.
25 : 11f.). The importance of this certainly should not be overlooked. In antiquity nations were taken into captivity from
time to time, as was about to happen with Judah. But nations
did not return from captivity. The whole point of transferring a
population was to break up the defeated nation and prevent it
from ever again becoming a threat. To allow it to return would
vitiate the whole exercise. From where then did Jeremiah get
the idea which clearly meant so much to him that the people
would come back? He said he got it from God, that God told
him (Jer. 32 : 36ff.). There is a note of certainty here which

is not accounted for if we reject the prophet's own explanation.

Another instructive incident in the life of this same Jeremiah is the occasion on which the army leaders with Johanan the son of Kareah asked him to intercede with the Lord. The leaders felt the need of divine guidance and thought that Jeremiah was the man to get it. Jeremiah agreed immediately. He was prepared to pray for them and he promised to keep in touch with them: "every word Yahweh your God replies I will tell you, keeping nothing back from you" (Jer. 42 : 4, Jerusalem Bible). But it was not until ten days later that Jeremiah got the divine answer (Jer. 42 : 7). He was not able to command the reply. He had to wait for it. Clearly it was not a case of his working the thing out and telling the others what seemed best as the result of his careful reflection. "Ten days later the word of Yahweh was addressed to Jeremiah." How it was addressed and how Jeremiah recognised it for what it was we do not know. Elsewhere this prophet speaks of being "present at the council of Yahweh" and asks, "Who has seen it and heard his word? Who has paid attention to his word in order to proclaim it?" (Jer. 23 : 18, Jerusalem Bible). This is tantalisingly brief. It does not enable us to say how Jeremiah knew that he (or some other prophet) had been in the Lord's "council". But it is clear that he saw this as a possibility that some men might attain. More. He saw it as the prerequisite of true prophecy. Only this enabled a man to declare authoritatively what God had said. It was because they had not stood in the Lord's council that the false prophets were in error. It was because they had stood there that the true prophets could set forth an authentic word from God.

It was evidently something like this with Moses. No prophet was quite like him, for him "the Lord knew face to face" (Deut. 34 : 10). Indeed, "the Lord used to speak to Moses face to face, as a man speaks to his friend" (Exod. 33 : 11). He is expressly differentiated from the usual run of prophets. "If there is a prophet among you, I the Lord make myself known to him in a vision, I speak with him in a dream. Not so with my servant Moses; he is entrusted with all my house. With him I speak mouth to mouth, clearly, and not in dark speech; and he beholds the form of the Lord" (Num. 12 : 6-8). This argues for close and exact knowledge of what God is saying.

Downing deals with this sort of thing only by saying that Moses had a special position and that it was not expected that the ordinary Jew would ever be in that position.[17] Once again we must counter that this is not the point at all. Of course Moses was in a unique position and nobody else would ever occupy that same position. That is not in dispute. But the question to which Downing does not address himself is, "Did Moses get real knowledge of God from that unique position?" And with it goes the further question, "If Moses did get real knowledge of God did he convey that knowledge, or some of it, to others?" If he really knew God and if he wrote what he knew, then we have revelation.

Moses and Jeremiah are examples of godly men who earnestly tried to find out what God was saying and convey it to others. There are also some instances of men who were not consciously trying to be vehicles of God's revelation, but who fulfilled that function in spite of themselves. The classic example is Balaam. His interest was in cursing Israel. When in the end he was not able to do this he gave Balak some advice as to how the nation might be defeated (Rev. 2 : 14) and in the end he died fighting against Israel (Num. 31 : 8). Clearly he was not giving his own best thoughts on the subject when in a series of oracles he proclaimed God's blessing on Israel (Num. 23, 24). This is a divine overruling. God has caused him to say what should be said and the words can scarcely be regarded as Balaam's own.

Something similar must be said about the unconscious prophecy of Caiaphas which John records (John 11 : 49f.). The high priest was speaking out of sheer political expediency and cynicism when he said, "it is expedient for you that one man should die for the people, and that the whole nation should not perish". It was not of his own will that he uttered words with a fuller and deeper prophetic meaning than he knew, words which applied to Jesus' atoning death for "the children of God".

This type of revelation is not common. Throughout the Bible by far the majority of those who spoke or wrote in the name of the Lord did so with full consciousness of what they were doing. But such passages as those just noted show that God is not limited by men's ability to grasp his meaning or their desire to set forward his purposes. He can, and sometimes does, use the most unlikely people to convey his revelation. Balaam and Caiaphas show that it is possible for God to make use of the utterances of men who do not realise the full significance of the words they are using and who certainly do not wish to set forward the divine purpose of which they are speaking.

These men were not prophets in the proper meaning of that term. But much in the Bible is spoken by the Lord's prophets and it is worthwhile accordingly to notice how they were regarded. At the time when Aaron became spokesman for Moses we read, "you shall speak to him and put the words in his mouth. . . . He shall speak for you to the people; and he shall be a mouth for you, and you shall be to him as God" (Exod. 4: 15f.). A little later we have this summary of the position: "See, I make you as God to Pharoah; and Aaron your brother shall be your prophet" (Exod. 7: 1). It is difficult to escape the impression that a prophet was regarded as a man who speaks the words that God puts into his mouth.

Mystery and Disclosure

There is good ground, then, for thinking that from time to time God has made revelations, mostly through people who cooperated with his purposes, but sometimes through men who were hostile. Now and then it is objected to the whole idea of revelation that if it did take place it would mean that there remains no mystery, no "hiddenness" in God. Man would know all that there is to Him. But this does not follow.

It is the consistent teaching of Scripture that man as such has no access to God's being. But this does not mean that man knows nothing about God. It means that the initiative remains with God. If he so chooses he can reveal himself. Of course it means also that if he chooses not to reveal himself man can do nothing about it. Sometimes discussions like those of Downing seem to imply that if a "hiddenness" remains then God has not revealed himself. But this does not face the possibility that God may choose to reveal something of himself to men while reserving his inner being. Men may know but "the outskirts of his ways" (Job 26: 14), though we should immediately add that those outskirts are well worth knowing. It is recorded that on Mount Sinai the Lord passed by Moses and proclaimed, "The Lord, the Lord, a God merciful and gracious, slow to anger, and abounding in steadfast love and faithfulness . . ." (Exod. 34: 6). Nobody will hold that this passage tells us all there is to know about God. There is mystery beyond it. But the point is that these words do tell us something about God. As they stand they are not a record of Moses's views. They are what God said to Moses about himself. Now if this is what happened the words record a revelation. The initiative is certainly with God. The disclosure of God's nature is partial.

He discloses what He wills to disclose, no more and no less. But the point is that it is disclosure.

Now and then this is expressed plainly in the Bible. When Paul is arguing that the Gentiles are blameworthy he bases his argument on the divine activity. "What can be known about God is plain to them," he writes, "because God has shown it to them" (Rom. 1 : 19). It is difficult to see what Paul can possibly mean unless that God has taken an initiative and revealed himself to the Gentiles of whom he is writing. God is active. It is true that the people in question did not respond to what God showed them, but that does not alter the fact that He showed it. Unless He had been seeking them and showing enough of himself to them for them to know that they should accept it it is hard to make any sense out of Paul's argument.

I do not see how it is possible for a Christian to reject the idea that God has disclosed at least something of himself and still be authentically Christian. In point of fact, many of those who raise questions about revelation seem to assume that something very like revelation has taken place. Thus we find Downing saying, "It is God loving first, and sending his Son, that makes real human love possible; God loving both elicits our love and makes it real."[18] This raises the interesting question, "How does Downing know this?" He dismisses the idea of revelation, and this makes the life of Jesus of Nazareth seem much like the life of any Galilean peasant of the time. Of course Downing may be prepared to argue that the teaching of Jesus and his miracles and the like *prove* him to be the Son of God quite apart from any concept of revelation. But I see nothing in his book that leads me to think that he would be prepared to take up such a position. And many recent writers, with a position not so very different from his about revelation, hold that there was nothing special about the life of Jesus, or at least nothing so special that the impartial observer would say, "This life proves that he who lived it was the Son of God."

I really do not see where Downing gets the idea that Jesus was the Son of God. Or that God sent his Son. Or that it is this that makes human love possible. If these things were revealed I could follow his argument. In fact because I do believe in revelation I accept what Downing is saying as true. But I cannot see how he comes to his conclusion on his own premises.

It is the same with his argument elsewhere. Thus he gently chides P. van Buren for not realising "how different the ethic of Christianity (and, less importantly, its 'understanding' of life) must become, if there is no 'gospel'." Then he goes on, "Just the attractiveness of Jesus in the Gospels, or in the whole New Testament and tradition, does not seem to me an adequate substitute for belief in the gracious activity of God."[19] But if there is no revelation to tell us of the gracious activity of God and if the attractiveness of Jesus does not tell us of it either, then how do we know that God is acting graciously? For a believer in revelation there is no problem, but I do not see how this can be established when the whole concept of revelation is abandoned.

Downing seems to use the language of commitment for such certainty as is obtainable. He prefers to speak of salvation rather than revelation and he can say: "The choice between 'salvation' and 'revelation' is between on the one hand a mythic understanding of and a committal to, a sequence of events that has happened and still happens, and on the other hand an equally mythic understanding of events that have yet to be found occurring anywhere, as the 'gracious activity of God'."[20] Those who hold that revelation has occurred will object strongly to his view that there has been a sequence of events for those who prefer to speak in terms of salvation but for those who talk of revelation only a mythic understanding of events "that have yet to be found occurring anywhere". There has been the same sequence of events whichever way we view them. Downing prefers to see a "mythic understanding" of certain events which calls him to commitment. Believers in revelation think that these same events happened whether we understand them mythically or not. And they see themselves called to commitment as fully as is Downing. They see themselves as the recipients of salvation just as surely as is Downing.

But they would go on to say that events that can do all this have some value as revelation. They tell us something about him who saves and who calls us to commitment.

Before we leave this section of our study we should look briefly at the fascinating question posed by Christopher Evans in the title of his book, Is "Holy Scripture" Christian? He concentrates on the three points "of the supposed apostolic origin of the New Testament, of the kind of exegesis which the concept of a holy book inevitably tends to produce, and of the genius of Christianity, if one might call it that, to secularise the sacred."[21] Under the first heading he draws attention to the fantasies that have been woven round the word "apostolic". He reminds us of the fantasy which lies behind Justin's view that the apostles proclaimed their message "to every race of men" and of that other fantasy which he puts this way: "As the oldest of them (i.e. the apostles) reaches his end the church, as it were, waits in suspended animation. He breathes his last; a gong sounds throughout the Christian world. The apostolic age is over, and the sub-apostolic age has begun."[22] I do not find this impressive. That members of the early church exaggerated the area visited by the apostles and that more recent members of the church have exaggerated the sharpness of the division between the apostolic and the sub-apostolic age are both true. But that does not affect the significant fact that it was the apostles and not someone else who bore the definitive witness to what Jesus did for men.

Evans's second point is the way the Bible has been interpreted in the church. He sees allegorical and typological methods of exegesis as arising because the Bible was thought of as a holy book. If its words did not appear to teach one and the same system throughout then those who saw it as holy held that it must be interpreted in such a way that it would. But surely it is not of the heart of the matter that some Christians have misinterpreted their Bible. That a wrong exegesis is possible does not carry the rider that a right exegesis is impossible. And as a matter of history there have been many believers who have thankfully accepted the Bible as what Evans calls "a holy book" and have proceeded to interpret it without either allegory or typology. Evans does not like the unity some people impose on the Bible. No more do I. Let the Bible speak for itself without our man-made unities. But that carries with it the further consequence that where the Bible has its own unity the exegete is not at liberty to deny it on the grounds that he perceives some diversity. If the evidence indicates both unity and diversity we must face it honestly without denying either the one or the other.

The third point seems to me the most important, though perhaps Evans does not see it that way, for he expounds it less fully than either of the other two. He holds that Christianity tended to do away with the category of the holy except as it applies to God and possibly also to the church. He sees this in the way Jesus largely by-passed Jerusalem, the holy city, and worked in Galilee. Paul refused to accept circumcision as necessary for salvation. "Holy" rites were not of the first importance. The Epistle to the Hebrews saw no need of temple, priesthood or sacrifice here on earth. Clearly Christians rejected much that in other religions was regarded as holy. It is the genius of Christianity to secularise the sacred. The implication is that the first Christians rejected the concept of a holy book.

This looks to me suspiciously like the *a priori* approach again. Before we come to the Bible we know it is not a holy book. To this I can say only, "Let the Bible speak for itself." It is not for us to decide in advance whether God has revealed himself or not, and, if he did, in what way he did it, whether in a book or in some other way. If he chose to do it in a book we cannot say in advance in what sense it will be "holy". We can only look at what has happened and let the facts speak for themselves.

NOTES

1. F. Gerald Downing, *Has Christianity a Revelation?* (London: 1964), pp. 47, 123 (Downing's italics).
2. Dr. Sigfrid Estborn, *The Expository Times*, vol. lxxxiv (1972–3), p. 325.
3. James Barr, *The Bible in the Modern World* (London: 1973), p. 36 (Barr's italics).
4. A. O. Dyson, *Who is Jesus Christ?* (London: 1969), p. 21.
5. *Ibid.*, p. 24.
6. *Ibid.*, p. 25.
7. James Barr, *The Bible in the Modern World*, p. 8.
8. *Ibid.*, p. 94.
9. *Ibid.*, p. 129.
10. F. Gerald Downing, *Has Christianity a Revelation?*, p. 89. Downing seems to admit the force of the passage for if it is late and Gnostic he allows that it may mean that Jesus reveals the "Father's identity, or, even 'self'" (*Ibid.*, p. 90). But if the words can have this meaning, they can have this meaning. The date does not come into it.
11. Dewey M. Beegle, *Scripture, Tradition, and Infallibility* (Grand Rapids; 1973), p. 25.
12. F. Gerald Downing, *Has Christianity a Revelation?*, p. 229.
13. *Ibid.*, p. 284.
14. *Ibid.*, p. 20.
15. A. O. Dyson, *Who is Jesus Christ?*, p. 27.
16. *Ibid.*, p. 120.
17. F. Gerald Downing, *Has Christianity a Revelation?*, p. 37.
18. *Ibid.*, p. 101.
19. *Ibid.*, p. 186, note 3.
20. *Ibid.*, p. 282.
21. Christopher Evans, *Is "Holy Scripture" Christian?*, p. 36.
22. *Ibid.*, p. 27.

CHAPTER 2

"General" and "Special" Revelation

TRADITIONALLY CHRISTIANS HAVE divided revelation into two categories, "general" and "special" revelation. General revelation is in the first place revelation made generally, i.e. revelation made to all men. It is not restricted to any one nation or group. And in the second place it is general in kind. It refers to the revelation that occurs in nature and in man himself. Special revelation, by contrast, is the name given to revelation in the Bible. Some Christians, of course, emphasise one of these at the expense of the other. There are believers who put little stress on the Bible, but who emphasise that God has made himself known in this world he has created. Others vehemently deny that any worthwhile revelation is open to man apart from that that God has made known in Scripture. A balanced approach sees both as having something to contribute to our understanding of revelation.

Revelation in Nature
The revelation in nature is the sort of thing that impressed the Psalmist when he sang, "The heavens are telling the glory of God; and the firmament proclaims his handiwork" (Ps. 19: 1). He saw this as happening by day and by night (v. 2). He refers metaphorically to creation as speaking (v. 4), but he is clear that "There is no speech, nor are there words" (v. 3). He has in mind a revelation of God inherent in the nature of things themselves. In a similar way Paul speaks of God's "invisible nature, namely, his eternal power and deity" as being "clearly perceived in the things that have been made" (Rom. 1: 20). Again at Lystra Paul and Barnabas are reported as saying that God "did not leave himself without witness, for he did good and

gave you from heaven rains and fruitful seasons" (Acts 14: 17).

Creation, then, gives evidence of its Creator. A reverent contemplation of the physical universe with its order and design and beauty tells us not only that God is but also that God is a certain kind of God. God has left his imprint on his creation so that his universe reveals something about him to men.

Especially is this said to be the case with man himself. The reasoning runs that if God can be said to have left his imprint on creation in general much more will this be the case with man, whom he made in his own image (Gen. 1: 26). The argument must be used with caution or else we find ourselves returning the compliment and making God in man's image. But those who use this line of reasoning suggest that qualities like personality, rationality and morality tell us something about the God who made man. Paul maintained that men have God's law written in their hearts (Rom. 2: 15). He is not talking about some restricted group, but about men in general. It is concluded from this that the moral sense found in all men points us to a moral God who made man in this way. While the precise deeds that men consider right and wrong vary, it seems to be universally agreed that some deeds are right and others wrong.

Sometimes this is discounted on the grounds that codes of morality vary so widely. There is some truth in this, but it does not get down to the impressive agreement among men in general in the kind of thing that is held to be right. For example, no society seems to think it right to be selfish. There are differences as to whether a man's unselfishness should be limited to the circle of his own family or extended a little to his own community or nation, or widely to embrace all mankind. But everyone agrees that selfishness is deplorable. So with killing. Men may hold that it is right to take life only by way of judicial execution, or they may extend it to war, or they may hold that killing is always wrong. But no society believes that it is right for any man to kill other men when and as he pleases. So with other aspects of morality. We should not minimise the extent of the differences. But those who argue in this way hold that there is enough in morality to tell us something about the God who made men moral beings.

Natural Theology
From time to time some Christians argue that it is useful or even necessary to develop a "natural theology", i.e. a theology based

solely on the revelation discerned in nature and not on the Bible. Sometimes a subordinate place is found for the Bible, but the emphasis is put on the importance of using one's reason on the phenomena of nature if one is to have a satisfactory religious life. Thus J. S. Bezzant says, "It is only by reference to a wider range of experience and knowledge than purely religious experiences that reasonable men can find *grounds*, as well as *causes*, for religious beliefs that can claim truth."[1] He is not saying that "purely religious experiences" have no value, but that more than this is needed if we are to establish a claim for truth. In line with this he further says,

> Intellectual objections to Christianity nowadays, in my judgment, and the fact that there are at present no convincing answers to them, both grow out of one root. This is that there is no general or widely accepted natural theology. I know that many theologians rejoice that it is so and seem to think that it leaves them free to commend Christianity as Divine revelation. They know not what they do. For if the immeasurably vast and mysterious creation reveals nothing of its originator or of his or its attributes and nature, there is no *ground* whatever for supposing that any events recorded in an ancient and partly mythopoeic, literature and deductions from it can do so.[2]

Bezzant is not arguing that Christianity is false. He is arguing as one who professes the Christian faith. But he is depressed at the neglect of reason he sees in some quarters. While he does not go so far as to claim that he himself can put forward the kind of natural theology that will win wide acceptance he is clearly of opinion that it is highly desirable that someone should do so. More, that it is possible. In other words, he is arguing that general revelation can give us a clear and sound base for our Christian faith.

Such views are strongly held by quite a few scholars, especially (though not exclusively) those in the "liberal" tradition. They hold that unless the Christian can draw attention to grounds for his faith (i.e. some evidence of God in the universe or in man) there is strictly speaking no *reason* for his being a Christian. To profess the Christian faith without such grounds they would hold is to make a choice for God on arbitrary, perhaps even on trivial grounds.

Some would go so far as to say that a right understanding of general revelation makes us independent of any ultimate dependence on the Bible. Thus F. H. Cleobury sums up the argument of his book in this way:

> The main contention of this book is that the work of one line of philosophical thinkers — the so-called neo-Kantian or neo-Hegelian idealists — has resulted in permanent advance. They completely shattered materialism and gave us a view of the relation of God to man such that our faith that God was in Christ no longer depends on our solving the historical question of the nature of Jesus's "claims" about himself.[3]

Cleobury maintains that it is only in the strictest sense that we cannot prove the existence of God. If we use the term "logical demonstration" in the sense of "offer a construction which will account for our experience", i.e. if we use the term "as we use it in science, in the law-courts and in the market-place", then he "must entirely reject" the view that "there are no logical demonstrations of God".[4]

This is an attitude that is far from common these days. But even unpopular opinions ought not to be rejected without close examination. While few will be prepared to go all the way with Cleobury, at the least he has made it clear that there is better evidence than is usually conceded that God has made himself known by the route of general revelation. There is certainly room for faith. God is not obvious. Many will not be convinced. But Cleobury makes the point that natural revelation provides more evidence about God than many today have thought. The revelation is real, if not coercive.

The Divine Initiative

The concept of general revelation is open to the objection that, taken at its face value, it seems to imply that there is a revelation running through the universe that is open to apprehension always and by all men in all places. It is doubtful whether the term "revelation" is properly to be used in this way. For this reason many prefer to speak of nothing more than the general possibility of revelation. The thought is that in nature and in man there is always the possibility of some revelation of God but that that revelation becomes actual only as God brings it home to some individual. The thought of the divine initiative is to be preserved. Revelation, by its very definition, does not mean something that is open to all men at any time. It is disclosure. It is God's being pleased to disclose himself. We may agree that He can do this and on occasion has done this through nature without the corollary that any man may become aware of the revelation whenever he chooses.

Some find it helpful to think of revelation as taking place on individual occasions rather than to speak of general revelation. The latter term may convey the impression that a continuous process of revelation is meant. What happens, it is rejoined, is that on occasion God takes a given situation in this natural universe and makes it the means whereby someone is led into an apprehension of truth. In this sense revelation is always "special", though it may make use of what is generally available.

This raises the question of what happens in natural revelation. The Psalmist could hold that the heavens declare God's glory and that the firmament shows his handiwork but every atheistic astronomer sees the same evidence and denies the conclusion. It can scarcely be held that the believer who sees the phenomena sees something physically different from that which any other observer (and even the believer in a non-revelatory situation) would see. To hold that would be a denial of the very idea of a revelation given in nature. The recipient of the revelation sees the same things, but he sees them in a different way. Perhaps as John Macquarrie puts it, he sees them in depth, sees "an extra dimension" in the situation.[5] He sees not only what the other man sees, but he also perceives what God is disclosing to him in the situation.

We ought not to think this so very surprising. In one way or another this kind of thing is common. The artist sees exactly the same landscape as the man who is oblivious to its beauty. But he sees it differently. He sees not only the trees and mountains and streams but he sees them as beautiful. Similarly in observing human behaviour some observers are more sympathetic and perceptive than others. All see the same things happening. But the sensitive take in more than do the careless. Examples of this sort of thing could be multiplied. There is no marvel in finding that some people have discerned God's revelation in situations where others have been blind to it.

John Calvin makes an important point in this connection in his treatment of the doctrine of the sacraments. He speaks of the rainbow set in the cloud which was to be a sign to Noah that God would not again destroy the earth with a flood. Calvin remarks that the rainbow "is merely a refraction of the rays of the sun on the opposite clouds" and could have no "efficacy in restraining the waters". Nevertheless

> that no one may suppose this to be spoken in vain, the bow itself continues to be a witness to us in the present age, of that covenant which God made with Noah: whenever we behold it, we read this promise of God in it, that he would never more destroy the earth with a flood. Therefore, if any smatterer in philosophy, with a view to ridicule the simplicity of our faith, contend that such a variety of colours is the natural result of the refraction of the solar rays on an opposite cloud, we must immediately acknowledge it, but we may smile at his stupidity in not acknowledging God as the Lord and Governor of nature, who uses all the elements according to his will for the promotion of his own glory.[6]

Here is the recognition that the bow occurs in accordance with certain natural processes. But with this recognition there is the claim also that God "uses all the elements according to his will". That is the claim also for natural or general revelation. It is not that there is any superlative merit in the researcher such that he is able to drag a knowledge of God from an unwilling nature. Nor is it that nature is there, brim-full of the knowledge of God for anyone who wishes to find it. The thought is rather that the sovereign God does what he wills with his creation. It reveals him in the way and to the extent that he wills that it disclose him.

It must be emphasised again that revelation is in the nature of a gift. Almost anything, it would seem, could be the occasion of revelation. Moses found a revelation of God in the burning bush, Joel in a plague of locusts, Amos in a plumb line. The Psalmist saw in the ear and the eye evidence that God hears and sees (Ps. 94: 9). Jesus spoke of God's care of the flowers and the birds. The possibilities are legion. But until God chooses to disclose himself they remain no more than possibilities. Revelation is an act of God, not man. All that man can do is to receive what God proffers.

The Recipient of Revelation

This does not mean that man's part in the revelatory process is unimportant. Unless he receives the revelation humbly and with faith revelation does not take place. We ought not to think of it as something given objectively in such a way that it

cannot but be seen and recognised for what it is. It can be misunderstood. It can be rejected. It is part of the orthodox understanding of natural theology that it does not and cannot of
itself bring a man to a saving knowledge of God. Natural
revelation shows a man to be the sinner that he is. It condemns
him. It does not necessarily enlighten him.

We must also bear in mind that it is part of this life that we
can never know beyond all doubt. Always the believer must
live in faith. Moses must believe that it was the voice of God
and none other that he heard in the bush that burned and was
not consumed. Isaiah must have faith that the voice that he
heard in the temple was the divine voice. The necessity for
faith exists equally for those to whom the revelation is passed on.
Men may still reject the revelation either in nature or in
Scripture or in both. Without faith there is no perception of
revelation. Not everyone who looks at nature or reads the Bible
is convinced. This does not leave the reality of revelation in
uncertainty. It is the perception of the revelation that is at
stake, not the revelation itself. God has spoken whether they
hear or whether they forbear. But unless men come in humble
faith they will still miss the wonderful thing that God is saying
to them.

Let me stress the need for humility in the face of God's
revelation and that in two ways. In the first instance it is
important that man be humble lest he feel that he has done
something wonderful in taking to himself the truth that God has
made known. In this matter he has nothing of which to boast.
He has done no more than receive a gift. And in the second
instance he should not think that he is, so to speak, in charge of
the revelation so that he can declare authoritatively where it
is going to lead. All too often in the history of the church men,
even holy men, have gone astray because they have thought
that they knew more about the implications of the revelation
than in fact they did. It will suffice to cite one instance, the
refusal to believe that the earth goes round the sun on the
grounds that the Bible teaches that the earth is the centre of the
universe. The Bible, of course, teaches nothing of the sort.
This is plain enough now. But it was not so plain in the days of
Galileo and that man of science was condemned by churchmen
who thought that they knew more about the implications of the
revelation than they really did.

This kind of thing is a perpetual call to men of faith to be
humble as they seek to relate the revelation to the circumstances

of their day. It is, of course, possible to go to the other extreme and be so ready to accommodate what the revelation says to what the best secular knowledge of the day has made known that the believer becomes hesitant and refuses to say anything without the consent of the secular authority. But somewhere in between is the middle ground that must be sought. Where God has spoken plainly, there what he has said must be accepted and obeyed. But we must always be on our guard lest we read our own ideas into the revelation and dignify the result with the title "the word of God".

There is a difference between the way we apprehend facts and the way we apprehend revelation. We elicit information about our universe by our own activity. We go out after facts and find them. In some quarters it would be objected that this is too strong a way of putting it. There is an element of "disclosure" even in the facts that our scientists make known. Some men of science and workers in other fields report that they have a feeling of having been gripped by the knowledge that has come to them, almost as though it was being "made known" to them. This has led some theologians to suggest that there is no great difference in principle between the knowledge that comes by revelation and that which men acquire by diligent research. But this is surely to go too far. There are very real differences between those who receive revelation and those who extend men's horizons by other means. There is a marked difference, for example, between the writings of Plato and those of the Old Testament prophets. Plato was a diligent seeker after truth and he has put all succeeding generations in his debt as he records what he learned in his search. But there is nothing in his writings equivalent to the "Thus saith the Lord" of the prophets. For the latter it is the disclosure that is the significant thing and this sets them and their revelation apart from other ways of apprehending the truth.

The disclosure aspect of natural theology must be carefully preserved or else the whole comes under the condemnation that it makes for the glory of man, not the glory of God. If God is "discovered" rather than "disclosed" then man may well claim the credit for an outstanding performance. But that is not the way it is in the Bible or in the history of Christianity. In both the knowledge of God is something to be wondered at. It is to be received with awe and gratitude, not self-congratulation.

Limitations of General Revelation

The value of general revelation is discounted by some who object that the best we can hope for from the revelation we see in nature is some information of an impersonal kind, a form of knowledge of little use to religion. The God men worship is personal and the information that is the end result of an impersonal process is at best of limited value. This may be freely conceded without denying that the impersonal revelation has its values. The essence of a right faith is the knowledge of God (John 17 : 3). But to know God does not mean that we must know nothing about him. It is quite possible to enjoy a vital, living communion with God and at the same time to rejoice in what we can know about him. We know about our friends as well as know them; why should it not be so in our experience of God?

Another objection to the whole concept of general revelation is that men cannot know God until it pleases him to reveal himself. "Can you claim to grasp the mystery of God?" asked Zophar (Job 11 : 7, Jerusalem Bible) and the answer of theologians like Barth is an emphatic negative. Any concept of God put together on the basis of natural religion is thought necessarily to be in error for it is the creation of man. Thus in his *Credo*, when he discusses the very first clause of the Apostles' Creed, "I believe in God", Barth lays it down that the very word "God" does not refer to "a magnitude, with which the believer is already acquainted before he is a believer, so that as believer he merely experiences an improvement and enrichment of knowledge that he already had".[7] He goes on to remark that when in Romans 1 : 19 Paul says, "that what can be known of God . . . is manifest to them, for God manifested it unto them, the whole context as well as the immediately preceding statement (Rom. 1 : 18) shows that Paul sees the truth about God 'held down' among men, made ineffective, unfruitful. What comes of it in their hands is idolatry."[8] Words could scarcely be stronger. Barth will have none of it.

But it is not only the Barthians who have difficulty with the concept of a deity who may be known by natural theology. R. Gregor Smith objects to our "inherited tradition of theological philosophising" for it "tends to locate God as the climax of a philosophical system, or as the conclusion of an argument designed to prove his existence". He contends that "Along such lines God can never be more than a thing within the world, or a speculative extension of the world" and he goes on to deal with what he calls the "fatal flaw" in this tradition.[9] Any view which leaves God as subject to man's will in this matter of man's attempt to discover what God is and is like must be rejected. It is important to let God be God and insist that man be seen in his littleness.

Herman Bavinck has a balanced evaluation of the values and limitations of general revelation. He sums up in these words:

> we discover, on the one hand, that it has been of great value and that it has borne rich fruits, and, on the other, that mankind has not found God by its light. It is owing to general revelation that some religious and ethical sense is present in all men; that they have some awareness still of truth and falsehood, of good and evil, justice and injustice, beauty and ugliness; that they live in the relationship of marriage and they live in the relationship of marriage and the family, of community and state; that they are held in check by all these external and internal controls against degenerating into bestiality; that, within the pale of these limits, they busy themselves with the production, distribution, and enjoyment of all kinds of spiritual and material things; in short, that mankind is by general revelation preserved in its existence, maintained in its unity, and enabled to continue and to develop its history.
>
> Despite all this, however, the truth remains, as St. Paul put it, that the world by wisdom has not known God in His wisdom (1 Cor. 1 : 21).[10]

Such a statement recognises that God has not left himself without witness. His general revelation has been productive in the life of man and Bavinck sees evidence of this on many hands. But the critical point is that this knowledge does not bring man salvation. Man does not come to know God as he is. When we reflect that general revelation gives us no information and can give us none about any of the central doctrines of the Christian faith we appreciate the limits of its usefulness. It tells us nothing of the Trinity, of the incarnation, of the atonement, of the person of Jesus Christ, of the person and work of the Holy Spirit, of the importance of conversion, sanctification and the like. All this must be conceded. But its silence about some topics should lead us to be deaf to its eloquence on others.

Special Revelation

The term "special revelation" is used to indicate the revelation recorded in holy Scripture. Here we may learn not only that it is God's nature to reveal himself, but that he has in fact revealed himself and the way in which he has done so. Man's knowledge of God comes from God himself. "God is known only as he speaks."[11] Special revelation is "given". It is not something that man has demanded, or even that the natural man, left to himself, recognises. It is, as Bernard Ramm puts it, "the knowledge of God adjusted for, and given for, sinners."[12]

It is "the knowledge of God". This does not mean that it is a full and complete knowledge of God. Earlier we were concerned to insist that the theologian does not have full knowledge of God as he is, and that the only knowledge of God open to him is that which God is pleased to reveal. But here we must insist that if this knowledge is partial it is still real knowledge. It is God and not someone or something less that is made known to us in special revelation.

This revelation came to men in a variety of ways. Sometimes it came in dreams or visions. There were oracles and on occasion the use of the sacred lot (Urim and Thummim, and cf. Acts 1 : 26). Sometimes "the word of the Lord came" to the prophets. Again, an object in everyday life might take on a new and profound meaning like the basket of summer fruit that Amos saw or Jeremiah's blossoming almond tree. Angels might speak. The Old Testament also records theophanies, direct manifestations of God. Again, history is the scene on which God works his works and history may thus be the means of revelation, interpreted as it is by the prophetic voice. There in no one way of God's making himself known. He acts with sovereign freedom.

Revelation occurs because God wills it to occur. Man does not control the process. He cannot decide that he will embark on such and such a process in the sure knowledge that in the end he will compel God to speak. God speaks when and as He chooses. God is not committed to man or to any place or any way of revealing himself to man.

It is special revelation that gives us the key to general revelation. Gordon H. Clark reminds us that "The ancient Babylonians, Egyptians, and Romans looked on the same nature that is seen by the modern Moslem, Hindu, and Buddhist. But the messages that they purport to receive are considerably different." He goes on to say, "What the humanist and logical positivist see in nature is entirely different from what the orthodox Christian believes about nature."[13] Without special revelation we would not know how to interpret general revelation. With it to guide us we can discern God's handiwork.

Special revelation has taken place in history, notably in connection with the history of the Hebrews. The history recorded in the Old Testament is real history, but it is recorded in terms of the outworking of the divine purpose. Behind the activities of the patriarchs, the events that make up the Exodus, the stories of the judges and the kings, the Exile, and all the rest, is Yahweh's sovereign purpose. Throughout there is the thought that God is active, and that He demands a response from his people. What happened in Israel's history is interpreted in terms of that response. The Old Testament does not suggest that history is the only medium of God's revelation. But it does make it plain that Israel's history, rightly interpreted, tells us about God, or, to put it another way, Israel's history is a means God uses to reveal himself.

The revelation reaches its climax in the life, death, resurrection and ascension of Jesus Christ. In him God is with us in a very special sense. But the process of revelation did not stop with the ascension. It went on in the life of the early church as it is recorded both in events (largely in Acts) and in interpretation (the Epistles and the Revelation). That revelation continued for some time after the decisive events in the work of Christ need not surprise us, for revelation includes interpretation as well as event and these events above all events needed interpretation. With the coming of that interpretation the need for this kind of revelation seems to have ceased. At any rate no more has been given. The closed canon is quite compatible with the inclusion of some books written after Christ.

The revelation is in both deeds and in words. Traditionally Christians have seen the revelation in the very words of the Bible, but in recent times many scholars have attacked the whole idea of verbal or propositional revelation. They prefer to think that God reveals himself in the mighty deeds that are recorded in the Bible, while regarding the words in which these deeds are recorded as not of primary importance. They see the writers of the books of the Bible as seized by the conviction that God has acted and as being anxious accordingly to record what God has done. But the revelation is in the deeds themselves and not in the record. For example, it would be said that God

revealed himself in whatever events underlay the Exodus story
but that the words in which the events are enshrined are not
specially important. In fact many scholars hold that the actual
events were very different from those we think happened if we
take the relevant accounts as straightforward narrative. That
God acted is not doubted. That the words in which God's acts
are recorded form part of the revelation is not only doubted
but rejected.

But this sharp separation between the words and the deeds
will scarcely hold. In the first instance, we have no access to the
deeds except through the record. If the record is unreliable then
we do not know what God did and accordingly we do not know
how he revealed himself. We have lost the revelation. And in
the second place, the interpretation given in the words' is a
necessary part of the revelation. We cannot doubt that the
events of the Exodus were seen by the Egyptians in a light very
different from that in which they appeared to the Israelites.
Were a contemporary Egyptian account to appear it is inconceivable that it would indicate that a revelation had taken place.

So with the constant teaching of the prophets throughout the
Old Testament period. They saw the hand of God in the events
that occurred in the history of their nation and the record of
their vision is the record of the revelation. A straight historical
account from the standpoint of a neutral observer would
scarcely rank as revelation. It is impossible to be rid of the
words if we are to find revelation in the deeds. It is the words
and the deeds which together make up the revelation. Only if
we can hold that God has inspired those who wrote so that they
put down the interpretation he wants men to have of the
events in question can we hold that the deeds are revelation.
The words and the deeds are bound up together. For real
revelation we need both.

Denial of Special Revelation
The whole concept of special revelation is denied by some who
put strong emphasis on the importance of the human approach.
Peter L. Berger, for example, (who calls himself a Christian,
though uncertain as to which heresy may rightly claim him!),
is typical of many when he emphasises the importance of discovery rather than revelation.[14] He repudiates the taking of
Christ's centrality as starting point:

I would take the historical materials concerning Christ, both the New Testament itself and the subsequent literature, as a record of a specific complex of human experience. As such, it has no special position as against any comparable record (say, the record concerning the Buddha in the Pali canon and the subsequent ramifications of Buddhist thought). The questions I would then ask would be essentially the same as on any other human record: *What is being said here? What is the human experience out of which these statements come?* And then: *To what extent, and in what way, may we see here genuine discoveries of transcendent truth?*[15]

This kind of approach may from time to time make a bow in the direction of revelation, but it concentrates on human achievement. It is interested in what man can discover, not in what God has made known. Such an approach (with all respect) smacks of human pride. To come to the Bible in this spirit is to decide in advance that God can have nothing to contribute worth knowing. Man is left to make all the discoveries he can. They are *his* discoveries. Man is now the measure of things.

Notice that this puts not man simply but modern man on a pedestal, for it cannot be denied that throughout the history of the Christian church it has been accepted without question until recent times that God has spoken and that it behoves man to take with the utmost seriousness what God has said. We cannot of course be bound by what our ancestors said and did. But it is a somewhat arbitrary procedure to lay it down that there is nothing in the all but universal Christian claim that God has in fact chosen to reveal himself.

It is better to sit humbly before the Bible and let it speak for itself. When it does it does not speak of the discoveries that men have made, at least not for the most part. By all means let us ask the questions of it that Berger poses. They are important questions. But let us also ask another: "Has God spoken here?" For the characteristic and distinguishing thing about the Bible is not the genuine human discoveries it records, but the fact that again and again it records its "Thus saith the Lord". Whether we accept it or reject it we should at least take the Bible for what it claims to be and not try to make it into something else which we like better.

The Truth of God
In view of the relativism of so much contemporary thought it is

worth emphasising the crucial importance of truth. It has well been said that by and large men today are more interested in what helps than in what is true, in what they are doing by way of works of love than in what they believe. This is the atmosphere in which we must live out our lives, the very air we breathe. It tends to make our generation impatient of serious discussions of what is true. It is apt to dismiss such inquiries as hair-splitting and to return with relief to the more congenial task of enjoying life.

But there is no sound basis for living (any more than for anything else) other than one anchored in what is true. If God has spoken then God's creatures ignore what he has said at their peril. We must not let the intellectual fashions of our day sidetrack us from the great eternal issues. There is a certainty about God's grace that we get from our day-to-day experiences. But there is also a subjectivity about it, for our experience may be susceptible of more than one explanation. It is well accordingly to reflect that our ultimate certainty of God's grace rests not so much on our own experience as on what God has disclosed of himself. Apart from this revelation we are left with our own imperfect understanding of what goes on in our experience (and in some measure in that of others). And the trouble with this is that there can be so many certainties. I may be certain that I am right. But my neighbour (whom I am certain is wrong) is equally certain that *he* is right. How are we to decide between our competing certainties?

The answer must lie in something external to both my neighbour and myself. In matters religious, certainty is given, not acquired. It is God's gift not man's achievement. It is divine grace not human merit. Man has no certainty apart from that which God pleases to give him. James D. Smart emphasises this. He notices that while churchmen try "to make God's authority visible, tangible, and incontestable" in fact "the authority of God's word everywhere in Scripture is invisible, intangible, and contestable".[16] We clamour for certainties of our own and we cannot get them. There is no substitute for living by faith and there never will be. Smart points out that Jeremiah "had no way of proving to his fellow Judeans that his word was in truth the word of God himself".[17] The same went for Paul and even Jesus. They were vigorously opposed even by religious leaders and they had nothing to which they could point that would give the certainty of irrefutable truth. All this must be accepted.

But the other side of the coin is that no man is wise to reject the certainties that God does give. If the Christian cannot be certain other than by faith, he can be certain by faith. He is not called upon to live out his life never knowing where he is, religiously. God does give what man needs, even if not what he wants. And in the Bible God has given such a revelation of himself that it is not the path of genuine humility to doubt it. Just as we must refuse to manufacture for ourselves a spurious certainty, so we must refuse to by-pass the certainty that God has provided.

All this means that the Bible has a special place. There is a "scandal of particularity" that we cannot evade. It is what God has done in Israel that matters not what he did in the nations generally, what he did in Jesus that is important not his action in men in general. It is in the death of Jesus that the atonement for men's sins was wrought out and not in the deaths of the martyrs who through the ages have lived and died for the truth. The Christian can never deny this uniqueness. It is integral to the Christian message.

But this means that he should never deny either the uniqueness of the book in which these teachings are enshrined. This does not mean that he minimises the values in other literature. Smart can say that we "find ourselves still without justification" in setting the Bible apart from "all other literature in which wisdom, moral courage, and spiritual insight are present".[18] But he also says, "the Bible is indispensable if we are to know God and if we are to be in truth the body of the risen Lord, because through it alone are we able to listen with Israel and with the apostolic church for the unique word out of the unseen which was for them, and can be for us, the power of God bringing our human life to its fulfilment."[19] I do not think that Smart is arguing for the same view of the Bible as I; nevertheless I endorse these words. We do not do justice to the facts, it seems to me, unless we see the Bible as unique in its testimony to the revelation God has given. We may well give honour to the literatures of many nations which present the virtues that matter so much to Christians. It is no part of the Christian way to denigrate such works. But it is no part of the Christian way either to overlook what God has done in giving us the Bible.

Smart warns us against another danger, that of picking and choosing in the Bible. He rejects the formula "the Bible *contains* the word of God", for the acceptance of this view puts a man in the happy position of being able to reject anything in Scripture that he does not particularly like. But "To eliminate the uncongenial may be to escape the judgment that makes us ready to receive the grace".[20] We must reject any idea of a canon within the canon. It is too easy a way of avoiding the challenge posed by the essential message of the Bible.

NOTES

1. D. M. MacKinnon, H. A. Williams, A. R. Vidler and J. S. Bezzant, *Objections to Christian Belief* (London: 1963), p. 106.
2. *Ibid.*, p. 107 (Bezzant's italics).
3. F. H. Cleobury, *A Return to Natural Theology* (London: 1967), p. 11.
4. *Ibid.*, p. 219.
5. John Macquarrie, *Principles of Christian Theology* (London: 1966), p. 80.
6. John Calvin, *Institutes of the Christian Religion*, IV, xiv, 18.
7. Karl Barth, *Credo* (London: 1964), p. 11.
8. *Ibid.*
9. R. Gregor Smith, *The Doctrine of God* (London: 1970), p. 146.
10. Herman Bavinck, *Our Reasonable Faith* (Grand Rapids: 1956), p. 59.
11. Bernard Ramm, *Special Revelation and the Word of God* (Grand Rapids: 1971), p. 144.
12. *Ibid.*, p. 20.
13. Carl F. H. Henry (ed.) ,*Revelation and the Bible* (London: 1959), pp. 27f.
14. Peter L. Berger, *A Rumour of Angels* (Pelican: 1971), p. 104.
15. *Ibid.*, p. 106 (Berger's italics).
16. James D. Smart, *The Strange Silence of the Bible in the Church* (London: 1970), p. 98.
17. *Ibid.*, p. 99.
18. *Ibid.*, p. 102.
19. *Ibid.*, p. 106.
20. *Ibid.*, p. 150.

CHAPTER 3

Christ and Scripture

FOR THE CHRISTIAN the critical thing in this whole subject is the attitude of Jesus Christ. He is the norm for the Christian and by definition the way he regarded Scripture is the Christian way. I do not mean by this that it is inconceivable that Christians will differ in the minutest particular from their Master. I mean rather that his attitude is definitive. With whatever minor modifications Jesus' view will be determinative for the Christian. If the follower of Jesus believes that Jesus was seriously astray in his view of revelation it is not easy to see the sense in which he is a follower. He is rather an independent critic.

It will not be possible for us to examine all the evidence about the way Jesus regarded and used Scripture. J. W. Wenham tells us that his examination of this general topic grew into a thesis of nearly a quarter of a million words, which he hopes to publish in four books: "The thesis of the whole tetralogy is that Christ's view of Scripture can and should still be the Christian view of Scripture."[1] We cannot here survey even the most important part of the mass of evidence. But we can indicate briefly what Jesus' general attitude was.

It is beyond all dispute that Jesus had a deep respect for his Bible. If the picture given in all four Gospels is only approximately accurate Jesus took the Bible as authoritative. This is not to assume that the Bible is authoritative and then deduce the same point from its pages by a process of circular reasoning. I am assuming nothing, but simply asking, "What do the available sources tell us about Jesus' attitude to the Bible?" The answer may possibly be that he saw it much as the modern critical scholar does, with some parts acceptable and some to be

rejected. Or he might ignore it and teach without regard to its
pages. There are other possibilities. I am not assuming anything
but asking what the evidence as we have it tells us about the
way he regarded his Bible, which was, of course, our Old
Testament.

In any discussion when he could say, "It is written—" that
apparently ended the matter. Take for example, the conclusion
to his parable of the wicked husbandmen: " . . . What then will
the owner of the vineyard do to them? He will come and
destroy those tenants, and give the vineyard to others." Jesus'
hearers interjected, "God forbid!" to which he replied, "What
then is this that is written: 'The very stone which the builders
rejected has become the head of the corner'?" (Luke 20: 15ff.).
This answer makes sense only on the presupposition that what
is written in Scripture is reliable. The end of his story is quite
reasonable, Jesus is saying, because there is a passage in the
Bible that bears on the situation. When that passage is quoted
and applied all discussion ends for Jesus.

Another instructive example is the way Jesus reacted to the
little story the Sadducees had about the lady who had seven
husbands in succession. For them the impossibility of saying
whose wife she would be in the resurrection was decisive. It
ruled out the very possibility of a resurrection. But for Jesus it
was the Old Testament that was decisive. He quoted the
passage which reads, "I am the God of Abraham, and the God
of Isaac, and the God of Jacob" (Exod. 3: 6) and commented,
"He is not God of the dead, but of the living; you are quite
wrong" (Mark 12: 26f.). The position of the Sadducees is for
him untenable. It did not accord with Scripture; therefore it
could not be accepted. This is all the more noteworthy in that
the inference that Jesus is drawing from the passage in Exodus
is not one which lies on the surface, to say the least. His argument could be used only by someone who trusted his Bible
implicitly.

Particularly important in this connection are the temptation
narratives. It might be urged that, in the cases we have looked
at hitherto, Jesus was simply using an argument that would
carry conviction to the men of his day, granted their view of the
Bible. But in the case of the temptation narratives this is not
possible. There was nobody present but Jesus and the tempter.
His quotation of Scripture under these circumstances points to
his own deep conviction. It is noteworthy that to each of the
three temptations Jesus said, "It is written" (Matt. 4: 4, 7, 10),

and that on every occasion that ended the matter. Scripture is final. Once its bearing has been discovered discussion is over.

This agrees with Jesus' habitual attitude to prophecy. He held that what the prophets had forecast would certainly happen. For example, in the synagogue at Capernaum Jesus said, "It is written in the prophets, 'And they shall all be taught by God'." He immediately added, "Every one who has heard and learned from the Father comes to me" (John 6: 45). It is written in the prophets. It will happen. Similarly he speaks of his rejection by the Jews: "now they have seen and hated both me and my Father." Then he explains it, "It is to fulfil the word that is written in their law, 'They hated me without a cause'" (John 15: 24f.). Sometimes the way prophecy is fulfilled is plain enough. But sometimes it is not, as when Jesus saw his resurrection on the third day foretold in Scripture (Luke 18: 31–3, 24: 45f.). Exegetes have had a notoriously difficult time in trying to identify the Old Testament passage or passages Jesus had in mind. Such a prophecy is not at all obvious. Only one who had the profound conviction that a thoroughly reliable Scripture predicted the chief events of his day would have discerned it.

The passion is of central importance in all four Gospels and prophecy is fulfilled in it. "The Son of man goes as it is written of him"; "You will all fall away; for it is written . . ."; "But let the scriptures be fulfilled" (Mark 14: 21, 27, 49). Jesus saw an overruling providence in all those happenings that would culminate in his death, and he saw that providence spelled out in the ancient Scriptures.

Luke records a saying of Jesus which brings before us the wide-ranging fulfilment for which Jesus looked. "Everything written about me", he says, "in the law of Moses and the prophets and the psalms must be fulfilled" (Luke 24: 44). He uses the threefold division the Jews saw in Scripture. The whole Old Testament in other words bears on his mission. Nothing is left out. All that is written must find fulfilment.

It is consistent with this that Jesus stressed the importance of Bible study. Negatively, its absence leads men into errors. Thus when the chief priests and scribes complained about the children crying out "Hosanna" in the temple, Jesus answered, "have you never read, 'Out of the mouth of babes and sucklings thou hast brought perfect praise'?" (Matt. 21: 16). Had they studied their Bibles they would not have made this mistake. So on another occasion he said to the Sadducees, "Is not this why you are wrong, that you know neither the scriptures nor the power of God?" (Mark 12: 24). It was this same essential attitude that he rebuked in the two who met him on the way to Emmaus, "O foolish men, and slow of heart to believe all that the prophets have spoken!" (Luke 24: 25). Clearly Jesus held that the Bible would not lead men astray. It is reliable.

Positively Jesus encouraged the study of the Bible. His general attitude comes through in the passages already noted. He was always quoting Scripture as final. And once he said to the Jews, "You search the scriptures, because you think that in them you have eternal life; and it is they that bear witness to me" (John 5: 39). This translation of R.S.V. is probably right, but the first verb could be taken as an imperative, "Search the scriptures". Sir Edwyn Hoskyns agrees that it is an indicative but goes on, "And yet, when this is said, an imperative lurks behind the indicative, for the Saying encourages the steady investigation of the Scriptures."[2] Jesus was not saying that they had studied the Bible too much, but rather that they had studied it too slightly. He was urging them to grapple with the meaning of the Scripture on which they put so much emphasis. His attitude may be further seen in some important sayings to which we now turn.

Notable Sayings
There are some notable sayings of Jesus which show his unfailing reverence for the Bible. It is recorded that in the Sermon on the Mount he said, "truly, I say to you, till heaven and earth pass away, not an iota, not a dot, will pass from the law until all is accomplished" (Matt. 5: 18). With this we should set another saying, "it is easier for heaven and earth to pass away, than for one dot of the law to become void" (Luke 16: 17). Such words indicate the permanent validity of the law. This term might refer to the first five books of our Old Testament which were (and are) the law *par excellence* for the Jews. But the term is used also with a wider sense to mean the Old Testament in general and it seems to be this wider sense that it has in these two passages. Both must be understood carefully, for the way in which the law is fulfilled may not lie on the surface. But for our present purpose the important point is not the precise manner of fulfilment but the fact of it in Jesus' teaching. He was clearly not allowing for the possibility that any man might set aside any of the law's teaching.

Once the Pharisees asked him a question about divorce to which he replied, "Have you not read that he who made them from the beginning . . . said, 'For this reason a man shall leave his father and mother and be joined to his wife, and the two shall become one flesh'?" (Matt. 19: 4f.). Now God is not said to be the speaker in the Old Testament passage Jesus is quoting. Some words of Adam are recorded and the narrator goes on, "Therefore a man leaves his father and his mother . . ." (Gen. 2: 24). It is difficult to see how this way of quoting Scripture can be defended except on the premise that what Scripture teaches, God teaches. Of course there are parts of the Bible of which God is not the author, things spoken by the devil, for example, or by evil men. But Jesus' words seem to imply that God is behind Scripture. Where we have positive teaching that can be regarded as coming from God.

Another illuminating passage is that in which Jesus defends himself from a charge of blasphemy in making himself God by citing Psalm 82: 6, "I said, you are gods". Jesus goes on, "If he called them gods to whom the word of God came (and scripture cannot be broken) . . ." (John 10 : 24f.). The Psalm is concerned with the judges and the term "gods" is used of them. Jesus' whole argument depends on the use of this term. Had another word been used it would have fallen to the ground. Yet it is of this passage, using one word rather than any of the others that might have described judges, that he says, "scripture cannot be broken." It is difficult to see how this can be explained other than on a very high view of the Bible. If such words can be used of such a passage then Scripture must be held to be reliable.

Sometimes it is said that Jesus' appeal to Scripture represents not his own thinking but his accommodation to the ideas of the men of his day. They had a high view of the Bible and the only way to convince them of the soundness of his position accordingly was to show that it was supported by Scripture. Though superficially attractive, this view will not stand serious examination. It does not account for Jesus' appeal to the Bible when he himself was tempted. Nor for the way he quoted Scripture when dying on the cross. At that time his use of the familiar words of the Bible could be only because they meant much to him, not because the bystanders would have been impressed. It is also the case that Jesus was not noted for being accommodating towards beliefs with which he was not in agreement. His denunciations of the Pharisees bring this out splendidly. Again, Jesus repudiated the nationalistic conceptions of messiahship that were so widely held in his day. Indeed, it would be difficult to find even one clear example of Jesus accommodating himself to currently held ideas about anything. In the end he went to the cross, partly at least, because of his steadfast opposition to the ideas held by leading men of his day.

Did Jesus Abrogate the Old Testament?

There is not much that can be set on the other side. It is pointed out that in the Sermon on the Mount there is a kind of refrain, "You have heard that it was said to the men of old. . . . But I say to you. . . ." In such passages, it is alleged, Jesus shows himself quite ready to jettison Scripture. But the force of this contention is diminished when we notice that in every such case Jesus takes Scripture further; he does not abrogate it. Thus when he takes the command, "You shall not kill," he does not say, "But now I authorise you to kill people" but on the contrary, "Don't limit this commandment too closely. You can break it simply by being angry with people." Similarly he extends the command about adultery to include the lustful look, that not to swear falsely to include unsworn statements. The rule limiting damages, "An eye for an eye and a tooth for a tooth," is extended so that one makes no demands whatever but turns the other cheek when injured.

Perhaps we should look a little more fully at this last provision for it is often cited as though it proved that Jesus quite specifically set aside part at any rate of the Old Testament. Here we should notice that in the ancient world there was one law for the rich and another for the poor and that this was taken quite literally and sometimes written into the statutes. For example, the Code of Hammurabi sets different penalties according to the rank of the person offended. If a citizen destroys the eye of another citizen his own eye shall be put out. But if it is the eye of a vassal he simply pays a mina of silver and if it is the eye of a slave he pays half his market value. An offence against a lord was in ancient times infinitely more serious than the same offence against a slave and the penalty varied accordingly. The Mosaic law is not rightly understood as a piece of primitive vindictiveness but "is properly seen as a significant advance, firmly and humanely limiting the imposition of damages: under this restriction the vindictive man of power is prevented from extorting exorbitant damages".[3] If we insist that the Mosaic Law was a piece of frightfulness and vindictiveness, if we hold that in all cases an eye must be put out for an eye then we will see a contradiction. But if we see it, as I think we ought, not as demanding that every eye should be recompensed with an equivalent eye but rather as limiting the maximum damages for an eye to an eye, then Jesus is simply taking this provision further in the manner of the other provisions in this section of his address. It is surely better to interpret the verse in a way which agrees with the context than to insist that it be taken otherwise.

Jesus then is not abrogating the law, nor giving his followers license to modify Scripture. He is filling out the implications of Scripture. In these verses, it should be borne in mind, Jesus uses an emphatic "I". He is not saying that anyone is at liberty to modify Scripture but only that he, being who he is and what he is, can do so. The words are evidence of a high view of his person rather than of a low view of Scripture.

Some see the abolition of the sabbath in Jesus' words, "the Son of man is lord even of the sabbath" (Mark 2 : 28). This is certainly a strong assertion of the greatness of his own person, but it is perverse to see in it any disparagement of the Old Testament. The right observance of the sabbath was certainly a point of controversy between Jesus and his opponents. But it is important to see what was at issue. On one occasion Jesus drew the attention of the Jews to the fact that they practised the Mosaic ordinance of circumcision on the sabbath if necessary (John 7 : 22f.) and used this as a justification of his sabbath healings. As I have written elsewhere:

> He was not arguing simply that a repressive law be liberalised. Nor did he adopt an anti-sabbatarian attitude, opposing the whole institution. He pointed out that his action fulfilled the purpose of the original institution. Had they understood the implications of the Mosaic provision for circumcision on the sabbath they would have seen that deeds of mercy such as he had just done were not merely permissible but obligatory.[4]

Jesus was not repudiating the Old Testament but asserting its true meaning. There is no more force in the contention that Jesus' quotation of Hosea 6 : 6, "I desire steadfast love and not sacrifice" (see Matt. 9 : 13), means abolishing sacrifice, a divinely ordained institution. This is the intention neither of Hosea nor of Jesus.

There is perhaps more in Mark's explanation that Jesus' words about defilement proceeding from within mean that "he declared all foods clean" (Mark 7: 18f.), for this does away with the distinction between clean and unclean foods, a distinction laid down in Leviticus. Jesus is certainly setting aside a provision made in the Mosaic law.

But are we to take this as a repudiation of the Old Testament or even as signifying that anyone is at liberty to set aside provisions of the law of which he does not approve? It is hard to think so. In the first place we should notice the context. Mark 7: 1-13 combines a strong attack on the tradition of the elders with a firm hold on the provisions of Scripture. It is not easy to think that the immediately following section is meant to teach that after all we need not hold to the provisions of Scripture.[5]

In the second place we should look hard at the meaning of the words. C. E. B. Cranfield explains them in this way:

> The key is rather that Jesus speaks as the one who is, and knows himself to be, *telos nomou* (Rom. 10: 4) – the one to whom both Law and Prophets witnessed in whom they find their fulfilment. As such a witness, the Law is that from which one jot or tittle shall in no wise pass away, till all things be accomplished (Matt. 5: 18); but now that he has come, who fulfils the Law both by being the one to whom it bears witness and also by fully obeying its radical demands, some elements of it (e.g. laws concerning sacrifices, circumcision, foods), though still valid as witness to Christ, are no longer binding in the sense in which they were before his coming.[6]

The coming of Jesus was decisive. The new way that he came to establish was not a mere carbon copy of the old. There was continuity but there was also radical novelty. Jesus built on the old but he also modified it where necessary, as here. But it is not easy to see how the making of all food clean is rightly to be understood as a blanket repudiation of the Old Testament. It is rather a filling out of that strand of Old Testament teaching which insists that "The earth is the Lord's and the fulness thereof" (Ps. 24: 1; Paul applied these very words to what may be eaten, 1 Cor. 10: 26).

The contention that Jesus selects his passages and does not put his *imprimatur* on the whole of the Old Testament proves nothing. Everyone who cites Scripture is selective, of necessity. It is impossible to quote the whole. What we do is to use those passages that are relevant to our purpose and pass over those that are not. We have no reason for thinking that Jesus did anything else. But with us the fact that we do not quote a particular passage at a given time (or for that matter over a period of time) does not mean that we do not regard it as authoritative. We may well ask whether it is any different with Jesus. In the nature of the case, some Old Testament passages were more relevant to his ministry than others. It is also quite possible that he personally found some passages of his Bible more appealing than others. But none of this implies any downgrading of passages that he does not cite.

The really important thing is that throughout the Gospels there is no equivalent of the attitude of some modern critics who find many parts of Scripture unreliable. Jesus never takes a verse from the Bible merely as a basis for discussion, nor as something that may safely be discarded. Throughout the Gospels his unfailing attitude to the Bible is one of respect. He handles it reverently as giving the decisive word.

Normative Scripture
It is important to notice that Jesus seems to have accepted the entire Old Testament without reserve. We today find difficulty with some passages that offend our tender susceptibilities. On this John Bright says:

> I find it most interesting and not a little odd that although the Old Testament on occasion offends our Christian feelings, it did not apparently offend Christ's "Christian feelings"! Could it really be that we are ethically and religiously more sensitive than he? Or is it perhaps that we do not view the Old Testament—and its God—as he did? The very fact that the Old Testament was normative Scripture to Jesus, from which he understood both his God and (however we interpret his self-consciousness) himself, means that it must in some way be normative Scripture for us too—*unless we wish to understand Jesus in some other way than he himself did and the New Testament did.*[7]

If we profess to be "Christians" then that surely means that we take seriously the attitude to the Old Testament that clearly meant so much to Jesus. It is hard to see what is meant by

calling ourselves "Christian" if we are to reject teachings that
were central to him. It is, of course, conceivable that a modern
man might wish to align himself with Jesus' general position
without binding himself to accept all that Jesus taught, and still
claim to be "Christian". But if he does this he can surely differ
from Jesus only on comparatively minor points. If he is to part
company with Jesus in matters which Jesus regarded as of
central importance, then it would seem that he ought to have
some better title for himself than "Christian". The unfailing
reverence with which Jesus regarded the Old Testament is not
lightly to be dismissed. As Bright says, Jesus took these writings
as normative and understood both God and himself from what
he read there. This cannot be dismissed as of no importance.
It is central for Jesus and I do not see how it can be rejected by
anyone who seriously claims to be his follower.

James D. Smart has a different idea about Jesus' attitude to
Scripture. Jesus, he thinks, "liberated God from his imprison-
ment in the tradition. He left behind no writing of his own, for
he himself had bitter experience of how Scriptures could
become a tyrant and a barrier against the living presence and
power of God."[8] This is an interesting view of the reason that
Jesus left no writings. It may possibly be the right one, though
I see no way in which it can be demonstrated. Jesus never said
why he did not write.

But there is one very significant thing to which Smart does
not direct attention. Granted his point that Jesus "had bitter
experience of how Scriptures could become a tyrant and a
barrier against the living presence and power of God", it is all
the more significant that he never advocated the abandonment
of the Bible. When we look at the fantasies of much rabbinic
exegesis we can discern a good case for saying, "If this is the
way Scripture is going to be handled let us get away from
Scripture." But Jesus never says anything of the kind. While he
saw that the traditions of the teachers of his day were alienating
men from the real God, hiding him away from them, he still
advocated the study of the Bible. He treated it with unfailing
reverence. Indeed, he did more. He said, "The scribes and the
Pharisees sit on Moses' seat; so practice and observe whatever
they tell you, but not what they do; for they preach, but do not
practice" (Matt. 23: 1f.). This is surely an endorsement of the
reverence the scribes and Pharisees showed for the Bible, whatever else it means. In view of the way the men of his day
treated the Bible this must be taken very seriously.

It is sometimes alleged that Jesus did not quote much from Scripture. It is not easy to see how this estimate is to be defended. R. T. France finds sixty-four "certain or virtually certain" quotations of the Old Testament or allusions to it in the words attributed to Jesus in the Synoptic Gospels.[9] This is no inconsiderable number, considering the length of the Synoptics. Equally impressive is the way Jesus made use of scriptural language even when he was not quoting. It has often been pointed out that there are few specific quotations from the Old Testament in the Sermon on the Mount, for example, but that it is permeated with Old Testament language and ideas. Nobody makes such use of Old Testament language unless the Old Testament has come to mean much to him. Jesus' usage is the result of prolonged study of and meditation in the Old Testament.

In recent years there has been an increased interest in typology and it is now widely accepted that this is a valid method of using the Old Testament. France has a long section on this subject.[10] He shows that Jesus not only quotes Scripture but finds certain individuals (Jonah, Solomon, David, Elijah, Elisha, Isaiah; also the nation, the priesthood) as types foreshadowing aspects of his ministry. He finds that Jesus "saw his mission as the fulfilment of the Old Testament Scriptures; not just of those which predicted a coming redeemer, but of the whole sweep of Old Testament ideas".[11] He differed from his contemporaries in France's view, "not because he took unusual liberties with the text (he was in general unusually faithful to its intended meaning), but because he believed that in him it found its fulfilment"; he was "second to none in his reverence for the Scriptures".[12] It is not easy to see how this conclusion can be disputed. Jesus had a fresh and original interpretation of the Old Testament. That is clear. But it is important to notice that it was an interpretation of the Old Testament, not a denial of it.

The Apostles and Scripture

The apostles had sat at Jesus' feet. They revered him as their great teacher. And it seems that they took over from him his approach to the Bible. It is, of course, possible that they were simply reflecting their Jewish heritage in their attitude to Scripture. But at least Jesus did nothing to disturb that attitude as he did disturb much that they had been taught. They looked at Scripture in the same way as he. We see the same unfailing respect for the Bible in their writings as in his teachings. They constantly cite Scripture and whenever they do they cite it as authoritative. They have the same readiness as Jesus to see a quotation from the Old Testament as settling a point under discussion and the same unquestioning acceptance of the view that whatever is written in the prophets cannot fail to be fulfilled. We saw that on one occasion Jesus attributed to God some words not specifically ascribed to him in the Old Testament. In the New Testament generally this phenomenon recurs. The New Testament writers cite the Old Testament as "God says", "Scripture says", "it says", or with the name of the human author, "Moses says", "Isaiah says". But however they cite it they always regard it as authoritative.

They have some striking things to say about Scripture. Let us notice but two of them. A very well-known passage assures us that "All scripture is inspired by God and profitable for teaching, for reproof, for correction, and for training in righteousness, that the man of God may be complete, equipped for every good work" (2 Tim. 3 : 16). Another tells us that "no prophecy ever came by the impulse of man, but men moved by the Holy Spirit spoke from God" (2 Pet. 1 : 21). Such passages raise their problems. But they are clear evidence of a high view of Scripture.

The attitude of the Christians to Scripture differed from that normally held by the Jews of the day. Sometimes this is taken to mean that the Christians had a lower view of the Bible. A. G. Hebert has a good summary of the objection:

St. Paul, writing to the Galatians, solemnly warns them that they must on no account undergo the circumcision which the Law commands; to the Romans, he says that there is no peace with God to be attained by the observance of the Law; in Ephesians, that the exclusion of the Gentiles from the privileges of Israel, symbolised by the Wall of Partition in the Temple, has been broken down. The readers of Hebrews are told that the day of the Temple sacrifices is over. St. John makes it clear that the Jews who reject Jesus are no true sons of Abraham. Behind all this lie the actions attributed to Jesus Himself in the synoptic gospels: He had broken the rules of Sabbath observance; He had called the Pharisees hypocrites; He had declared the laws of ritual uncleanness to be no longer binding, annulled the Mosaic permission for divorce, and had performed, as the last act of

His ministry, a rite, independent of the levitical sacrifices, in which He had declared the New Covenant to be inaugurated through His blood.[13]

All this, however, amounts to not much more than a recognition that in the coming of Jesus a new situation has developed. He is the fulfilment of all that the Old Testament foreshadows. It is basic to the New Testament that it is Jesus' death that brings men salvation. That is why Paul warns the Galatians against undergoing circumcision. Having accepted salvation as Christ's free gift they must not undergo a rite which means the acceptance of an obligation to perform the whole law. To do that would be to see law and not grace as the way of salvation. So with his words to the Romans and Ephesians. If peace came by Christ then it does not come by the law. The end of the Temple sacrifices in Hebrews means a recognition of the same truth. The point from John about being true sons of Abraham arises from the truth insisted upon throughout the New Testament that the way of faith that Abraham trod is the way Christians must go, for Abraham rejoiced at Jesus' day (John 8: 56). In fact we could sum up all the passages so far noted under the rubric that the law is a schoolmaster to bring us to Christ (Gal. 3: 24).

As for the passages about Jesus, I doubt that it can be shown that he "had broken the rules of sabbath observance", i.e., if "the rules" means the teaching of the Old Testament. He broke the regulations the Pharisees laid down, but the position taken up by the Evangelists is that he fulfilled the true meaning of the sabbath (Luke 6: 9, John 7: 23). Calling the Pharisees hypocrites can scarcely be said to contradict the Old Testament and again I do not think it is true that Jesus "annulled the Mosaic permission for divorce". He declared the true meaning of marriage, but New Testament exegetes differ widely as to the extent to which he limited divorce.[14] It cannot be said that he contradicted Moses. The establishment of the new covenant, and of the Holy Communion which celebrates it, can scarcely be said to be in violation of the Old Testament which explicitly looks forward to the new covenant. And, of course, the laws on ritual uncleanness must be seen in the light of the meaning of the new covenant.

I do not mean that there are no problems in the Christian attitude to the Old Testament, nor that the passages to which Hebert draws attention do not demand careful scrutiny. But that they mean that the early Christians repudiated the Old Testament must be decisively rejected. They represent no more than the inevitable working out of the New Testament view that there is both continuity and discontinuity with the old dispensation. As Herbert puts it when he finishes his examination of the passages he lists, "When all irrelevances are cleared away, as they need to be, there is one outstanding question, and one only, between Christians and Jews. It is the question whether God did or did not accomplish in Jesus His purpose of Salvation for Israel."[15] If Jesus is indeed the Messiah foretold in the Old Testament then the difference between the early Christians and contemporary Jews are accounted for. And the Christians are certainly affirming the authority of the Scriptures that foretold the coming of their Messiah.

The New Testament
So far we have been looking only at the attitude of the men of the New Testament to the Old Testament. But they have something to say about their own writings, too. Perhaps we should start with the fact that Jesus himself said, "Heaven and earth will pass away, but my words will not pass away" (Luke 21 : 33). Again, there are places where it is said that his word must be fulfilled, quite in the manner of the fulfilling of the Old Testament (e.g. John 18: 32). It is clear that the words of Jesus are regarded as in no way inferior to the Old Testament.

Of the New Testament writers in general perhaps B. B. Warfield has said what needs to be said as well as anyone : the New Testament writers

> freely recognise, indeed, that they have no sufficiency of themselves, but they know that God has made them sufficient (2 Cor. 3 : 5, 6). They prosecute their work of proclaiming the gospel, therefore, in full confidence that they speak "by the Holy Spirit" (1 Pet. 1 : 12), to whom they attribute both the matter and form of their teaching (1 Cor. 2 : 13). They, therefore, speak with the utmost assurance of their teaching (Gal. 1 : 7,8) ; and they issue commands with the completest authority (1 Thess. 4: 2, 14; 2 Thess. 3: 6, 12), making it, indeed, the test of whether one has the Spirit that he should recognise what they demand as commandments of God (1 Cor. 14: 37). It would be strange, indeed, if these high claims were made for their oral teaching and commandments exclusively. In point of fact, they are made explicitly also for

their written injunctions. It was "the things" which Paul was "writing", the recognition of which as commands of the Lord, he makes the test of a Spirit-led man (1 Cor. 14: 37). It is his "word by this epistle", obedience to which he makes the condition of Christian communion (2 Thess. 3: 14). There seems involved in such an attitude toward their own teaching, oral and written, a claim on the part of the New Testament writers to something very much like the "inspiration" which they attribute to the writers óf the Old Testament.[16]

We should add that Paul's regulation of the way believers should exercise the gifts of the Spirit of God (1 Cor. 14) is surely evidence of a deep conviction that what he said was divinely inspired (and in this context he draws specific attention to the things he is writing, 1 Cor. 14: 37). The new covenant is a "better" covenant, as the Epistle to the Hebrews says more than once. It spoke of a salvation which was "declared at first by the Lord, and it was attested to us by those who heard him, while God also bore witness by signs and wonders and various miracles and by gifts of the Holy Spirit" (Heb. 2:3f.). It is difficult to think that the writings telling of such a salvation are inferior to those of the lesser covenant. We could draw a similar conclusion from the end of Romans. Here we read of Paul's gospel "and the preaching of Jesus Christ, according to the revelation of the mystery which was kept secret for long ages but is now disclosed and through the prophetic writings is made known to all nations" (Rom. 16: 25f.).

The Subapostolic Church
It is worth noticing that the writers of the early church differed from the apostles in the way they viewed their writings. As we have just seen, the apostles write with complete authority and make it clear that they expect their writings to be treated with the greatest respect. The next writers are a complete contrast. They see themselves simply as members of the church, as equals writing to equals, and they view the writings of the apostles as something very different. Clement of Rome, for example, writing towards the end of the first century, does not even use his name but begins, "The Church of God which sojourns in Rome to the Church of God which sojourns in Corinth."[17] He does not distinguish himself from the rest of the church. Later he says to his readers, "we are not only writing

these things to you, beloved, for your admonition, but also to remind ourselves; for we are in the same arena, and the same struggle is before us" (7:1). But when he is referring to Paul he says, "Take up the epistle of the blessed Paul the Apostle. . . . With true inspiration he charged you concerning . . ." (47:1-3).

The date of the Epistle of Barnabas is uncertain, but it is agreed that it is late first century or early second century. This writer ventures to write "not as a teacher but as one of yourselves" (1:8); "And this also I ask you, as being one of yourselves" (4:6). It is not in this strain that the men of the New Testament convey their teachings to their readers.

Polycarp (early second century) was highly esteemed in his day, and for that matter in subsequent generations. But he sees himself as on a different footing from the apostles. He writes to the Philippians:

> For neither am I, nor is any other like me, able to follow the wisdom of the blessed and glorious Paul, who when he was among you in the presence of the men of that time taught accurately and stedfastly the word of truth, and also when he was absent wrote letters to you, from the study of which you will be able to build yourselves up into the faith given you" (Phil. 3:2).

In the same spirit he urges his readers to serve the Lord "as he himself commanded us, and as did the Apostles" (6: 3). From time to time he quotes the apostolic writings and once cites Ephesians as Scripture (12: 1). It is instructive to notice that he refers also to the writings of Ignatius. Evidently the Philippians had asked him for any letters of the martyr in his possession and he sends them copies (13: 2). Quite plainly Polycarp esteemed these letters highly. But equally plainly he did not put them on the same level as the writings of Paul.

Ignatius makes the same distinction. "I do not order you", he writes to the Romans, "as did Peter and Paul; they were Apostles, I am a convict" (Rom. 4: 3). To the Trallians he says much the same, "I did not think myself competent, as a convict, to give you orders like an Apostle" (Trall. 3: 3). His reference to himself as a convict should not be misunderstood. He was not a criminal, but one convicted of the offence of being a Christian. But his status as a martyr-elect did not permit him to class himself with the apostles. They were different. As is well known, Ignatius lost no opportunity of putting the clergy in a high place. For our present purpose it is worth noticing that in the process he sometimes gives evidence of classing the apostle with Christ over against all others. Thus he writes to the Magnesians, "As then the Lord was united to the Father and did nothing without him, neither by himself nor through the Apostles, so do you do nothing without the bishop and the presbyters" (Mag. 7:1); "Be zealous to do all things in harmony with God, with the bishop presiding in the place of God and the presbyters in the place of the Council of the Apostles" (Mag. 6:1).

It is scarcely necessary to proceed further. Others could be cited but it would be to the same effect. These early Christians saw the place of the apostles as essentially different from their own. When they refer to their writings it is always as to authoritative documents which differ from the writings of their own day.

A Biblical Faith

Even so quick a survey as this is sufficient to show that Christ and his apostles did indeed have a high regard for Scripture. They treated it with respect and they always regarded it as authoritative.

We can say more. A. G. Hebert thinks that we ought to be disturbed to find that our presentation of the faith differs so radically from that of the early Christians. He points out that we are very likely to hear in any sermon on the Passion, for example, a psychological study of one or other of the participants in the story and at Easter something similar or perhaps a doctrinal study of the atonement or of the resurrection of the body. But the men of the New Testament were different:

> the striking feature of their handling of these subjects, and the point at which they differ from the modern preacher, is that they are continually referring to the Old Testament, either by quoting it directly, or by alluding to it in their choice of phrases; and it is by use of the Old Testament that they habitually explain the meaning of the events which they are describing.[18]

There is a whole attitude to the faith at stake here. The men of the New Testament were proclaiming a biblical faith. They saw God as having revealed great truths in the sacred books.

They saw it as important in setting forth the faith by which they lived and were to die that they were not producing some bright idea of the latest first-century whizz kid but proclaiming what God had done in accordance with his revelation from of old. We may or may not need to cite Scripture in quite the way they did. But if we lose their certainty that God had acted in Christ in accordance with Scripture we lose a highly significant element in the faith of the New Testament church. Revelation is not to be denied.

NOTES

1. J. W. Wenham, *Christ and the Bible* (London: 1972), p. 7.
2. Sir Edwyn Hoskyns, *in loc.*
3. B. D. Napier, *Exodus* (London: 1963), p. 98.
   H. Cunliffe-Jones has a comment on the equivalent provision in Deuteronomy: "It is well to remember that it represents an advance on what went before it. It puts an end to the interminable continuance of blood-feud, each new requital starting a new act of retaliation, and it put an end to| the repayment of injuries with interest' (*Deuteronomy* (London: 1951), p. 118).
4. Leon Morris, *The Gospel according to John* (Grand Rapids: 1971), p. 409.
5. B. H. Branscomb denies that Jesus "abrogated the food codes of Leviticus". He prefers to understand the saying in the light of Jesus' acceptance of the Sabbath while rejecting the way the Jews understood it. "He may very well have decided, in connection with some specific case that arose, that a good man who was engaged in doing a good deed did not become evil in God's sight through the food which he ate" (*The Gospel of Mark* (London: 1946), p. 126). Personally I think the words go further, but Branscomb's denial that Jesus abrogated the Levitical code is interesting.
6. C. E. B. Cranfield, *The Gospel according to Saint Mark* (Cambridge: 1959), pp. 244f.
7. John Bright, *The Authority of the Old Testament* (Nashville: 1967). pp. 77f.
8. James D. Smart, *The Strange Silence of the Bible in the Church* (London: 1970), p. 146.
9. R. T. France, *Jesus and the Old Testament* (London: 1971), p. 27.
10. *Ibid.*, pp. 38–82.
11. *Ibid.*, pp. 79f.
12. *Ibid.*, pp. 201, 223.
13. A. G. Hebert, *The Authority of the Old Testament* (London: 1947), p. 200.
14. Cf., Hugh Montefiore, "It is not possible to ground the judgment that all divorce and remarriage is forbidden on the fact that Jesus definitely forbade it. He may not have done so—many, perhaps most, would say he most probably did not" (*Marriage, Divorce and the Church*, The Report of a Commission appointed by the Archbishop of Canterbury to prepare a statement on the Christian Doctrine of Marriage (London: 1972), p. 95).

15. A. G. Hebert, *The Authority of the Old Testament*, p. 238.
16. B. B. Warfield, *The Inspiration and Authority of the Bible* (London: 1951), pp. 163f.
17. The translations in this section are all from the Loeb edition.
18. A. G. Hebert, *Scripture and the Faith* (New York: 1962), p. 13.

CHAPTER 4

Formative Revelation

MANY CHRISTIANS REPORT personal and individual experiences in which they say that God has spoken to them. Some believers appear to have constant experience of divine guidance as they live out their faith. Somewhere I recall reading that Archbishop Temple testified that from time to time he had the experience of feeling that he ought to go and see someone and that when he responded he was often able to render significant spiritual help. He added that when his own spiritual life was not in good shape he had these experiences more rarely.

That individual Christians have such direct contact with God and receive what they take to be divine guidance directly from him is not to be doubted. And since on occasion this represents the communication of knowledge and guidance it is not inappropriate to speak of "revelation" as taking place. But clearly this is something quite different from the kind of revelation of which we have been speaking up till now. That kind of revelation is not private, but one which concerns the whole Christian community. It has the characteristic of being definitive for the Christian church and not simply an aid to Christian living. John Macquarrie has a helpful thought when he refers to this type of revelation as "primordial revelation". This he sees as wider than Christianity and as having relevance to almost any religious group.

> A community of faith, within which a theology arises, usually traces its history back to what may be called a "classic" or "primordial" revelation. This classic revelation, a definitive disclosive experience of the holy granted to the founder or founders of the community, becomes as it were

the paradigm for experiences of the holy in that community. A revelation that has the power to found a community of faith becomes fruitful in that community, and is, so to speak, repeated or re-enacted in the experience of the community, thus becoming normative for the experience of the community. Yet only because the primordial revelation is continually renewed in present experience can it be revelation for us, and not just a fossilized revelation.[1]

A little later Macquarrie underlines the importance for all time of the primordial revelation by saying,

if theology is to be saved from the dangers of subjectivism, the varieties of experience within the community must be submitted to the relatively objective content of the classic revelation on which the community is founded.[2]

In other words, the primordial revelation sets the general course for all time of the community of faith for which it is definitive. This does not mean that there can be no progression. With Macquarrie we protest against "a fossilized revelation". It is not thus that the Christian regards his Bible. Nor does it mean that there can be no diversity. The most cursory glance at the history of Christianity reveals that there has been wide diversity in the way the Bible has been understood, a diversity in which more than one group can claim to have been faithful to Scripture. In a book as diverse as the Bible it is quite possible for some to emphasise one aspect and others another while both are basing their teaching on the deposit of revelation. I am not arguing that the idea of a primordial revelation means a monochrome Christianity. I am simply saying that there are limits to what can be called authentic Christianity and that these limits are indicated by the Bible. Any advance that can claim to be authentically Christian will be in accordance with and not in contradiction of the primordial revelation. If the community of faith goes off in a direction not sanctioned by the primordial revelation it becomes something other than it professes to be and it forfeits its right to its original name and function.

For Christians the primordial revelation is that contained in the Bible. It is not only the books containing the deeds and words of Jesus, but the Old Testament and the other books of the New Testament as well. Here are the decisive events and teachings on which Christianity was founded. Anything that claims to be Christianity must be authenticated by reference to this primordial revelation. If its claim can be made out by this referral then it is the genuine article. If it cannot, it has no right to the name.

Throughout the history of the Christian church, times of spiritual zeal and times of spiritual slackness have alternated. Sometimes men with curious ideas have tried to have them accepted as authentically Christian. Now and then they have succeeded in some measure. The classic illustration is that time in the Arian controversy when, in Jerome's famous epigram, "The whole world groaned and marvelled to find itself Arian."[3] The triumph of Arianism seemed secure. But subsequent generations of Christians have found Arianism heretical and condemned it as unchristian. It is out of harmony with the primordial revelation. Other times of doctrinal error and spiritual slackness have likewise been succeeded by times of renewal when men rediscovered what the primordial revelation teaches. It brings men back to that essential teaching that makes Christianity what it is.

"Repetitive" Revelation

Of course the revelation must become real to generation after generation of Christian people. Here what Macquarrie calls "repetitive" revelation is important. He takes the concept of repetition from the existentialists and sees it

> as meaning much more than a mere mechanical going over again. It implies rather going into some experience that has been handed down in such a way that it is, so to speak, brought into the present and its insights and possibilities made alive again.[4]

This repetition is not limited to any one form from the past. It can occur in connection with a historical happening or a saying or a poem. It is essential that it happen with revelation, for the modern believer is not simply appealing to something from a remote antiquity that has the character of an external, objective proof of some position that he wishes to take up. Rather he sees it as something which is alive and vital for him in his own situation. There is an inner witness of the Spirit of God with his own spirit that assures him that this is indeed so. The revelation is not simply something he has heard about or even read for himself. He has been gripped by it. It is real and relevant. It confronts him with an authority from which he knows there is no appeal. He submits to it for he receives it as indeed God's word. There is an inner compulsion he cannot escape.

When this "repetitive" revelation takes place the modern believer finds himself heir to the ages. He receives not only the primordial revelation but also the reflection of the Christian generations on that revelation. Of course this presents him with a problem, for it is always possible for those subsequent generations (including his own) to go astray as they try to bring out the implications of the classic revelation. He must always sift the tradition to see what is of God and what is of men. But it is an important part of the living out of the faith that in any later day the believer is the heir not only to the primordial revelation itself, but also to the thought and experience of those who have lived the Christian life and interpreted the Christian way before him.

Tradition
This raises the question of the relation of Scripture to tradition, and of both to the revelation. Many scholars emphasise that the revelation is one thing, the record of it quite another. They draw the corollary that we should give earnest heed to the revelation, but not have quite so much respect for the Bible which enshrines it or for the tradition by which we interpret it.

Now it must of course be accepted that it is what God has revealed that is important. The wrappings in which it comes do not matter in comparison with the precious deposit of truth. It is obviously more important that we come to know God than that we come to know the Bible. But the question must be asked, "How are we to know the revelation apart from the Bible?" It is in this book and in this book alone that we have our record of the revelation. It is true that some in these days do not like an exclusive emphasis on the Bible. I am not at this point arguing against their position. I am simply pointing out that there is no other claimant for the primordial revelation than the Bible. Other Christian writings have come down to us from antiquity but, as we saw earlier, their writers sharply differentiate them from the writings of the apostles. There is no other source for the revelation than the Bible. If the Bible cannot lead us to the revelation nothing can. In their anxiety to avoid fundamentalism many scholars seem to have missed this point or at least to have underestimated its significance. It is one thing to recognise the excesses in fundamentalism and quite another so to exalt the critical method that it is difficult if not impossible to discover what the revelation is.

Scripture provides us with an objective point of reference. It enshrines the "faith once delivered to the saints" and enables the church at any subsequent time to compare its life and teaching with that of the earliest church. It forms the church's memory cells, so that when aspects of the truth are neglected or forgotten they may be recovered by diligent study of the foundation documents. When we reflect on the great variety of temperaments, outlook, culture and the like that are represented in the Christian church as well as the different ideas that have been accepted through the centuries it is well that there should be this objective standard. The Bible is always calling the church back to fundamentals.

But of course the Bible is never interpreted in a vacuum. It is the church's book and it is read in the Christian community. This means that there are traditional ways of interpreting it and we cannot ignore them. There is a classic difference of opinion between Catholicism and Protestantism in this matter of tradition, though it must be added that the gap is not as wide these days as it has been. But it cannot be denied that some in the Catholic tradition have made tradition a source of Christian doctrine on a level with Scripture. Others have regarded Scripture as simply part of tradition. In practice this has often meant that Scripture is subordinate to tradition, for it is the way the church interprets Scripture that is decisive. It becomes impossible in this situation to appeal to the Bible against the church, for when the reformer cites Scripture against the church's teaching or practice he is told that he cannot be interpreting Scripture in the right way. Anything that conflicts with the church's interpretation is *ipso facto* ruled out.

It becomes possible on this view of the church and tradition for new dogmas to be accepted with no warrant in Scripture, for example the Roman Catholic doctrine of the Assumption of the Blessed Virgin Mary. It is true that the Roman Church officially accepts the supremacy of Scripture. But, as the promulgation of this dogma shows, when tradition is held to be of equal weight with the Bible the result must be the supremacy of tradition. Christopher Evans underlines the problem when he speaks of "more recent dogmas pronounced by the Church of Rome" in which "the place of traditions is taken by tradition, understood now as that which is believed by the present consensus of the faithful". Of this view he says, "It is difficult to exaggerate the horror of the Protestant at the possibilities of corruption inherent in this vicious circle, whereby the Scriptures are deprived of their power to purify the Church because they are made always to echo the voice of the Church."[5]

It is true that some Roman Catholics are now modifying the older position. Thus Karl Hermann Schelkle repudiates views which see Scripture and tradition as independent streams or which see tradition as contributing something "essentially new". "Rather, it means that we have *one* stream by means of which Scripture is passed on to the Church through living tradition, and freshly presented in every new epoch."[6] This is to be welcomed, but it cannot be held to represent the current Roman Catholic position. And where the view opposed by Evans flourishes it must continue to be opposed.

We have referred to the view that Scripture is itself part of the church's tradition, a view with many adherents these days. Evans puts it this way: "For it is not now the Bible and tradition alongside each other, or over against each other, but tradition within the Bible, the Bible itself largely tradition."[7] I imagine that almost everything here hinges on what we mean by tradition. Nobody doubts that for a time the content of the Gospels was handed down orally in the Christian church, i.e., by tradition. There is a sense in which we can speak about pretty well everything in the Gospels, and a good deal beside, as "tradition". And we must bear in mind that now and then the Christians can use the term in a good sense, as when Paul enjoins the Thessalonians to keep away from any brother "who is living in idleness and not in accord with the tradition that you received from us" (2 Thess. 3 : 6).

But we must also bear in mind that in the New Testament generally "tradition" has a nasty sound. It is that by which the Jewish opponents of Jesus made the word of God void (Mark 7 : 13), and that by which false teachers might "make a prey" of the Colossian Christians (Col. 2 : 8). Obviously it will not do simply to label the Bible with a label which for the most part it repudiates. If by tradition we mean essentially a human process and that the tradition in the Bible is much like any other tradition then the usage seems condemned by the Bible itself. It is acceptable only if it is seen as a human process indeed, but one in which God is concerned, and concerned in such a way that he has made the result to be the authoritative tradition.

A further problem about tradition is that those groups of Christians who stress it most seem to draw quite divergent conclusions from it. Thus the Roman Church differs in not unimportant ways from the Orthodox and both differ from the Anglo-Catholics. Some tradition must be wrong. The idea works out badly in another way, too. While the general positions of the churches which stress it are fairly clear it is not so clear what interpretations they are giving of biblical passages (other than a small handful). If we ask for the official interpretation of a passage that is giving us trouble we are likely to find it hard to get a clear answer. The number of passages on which an authoritative pronouncement has been made is small.

The Voice of the People
We may consider next a view which is not usually put into so many words but which appears to mean that what the majority of those who profess Christianity at a given time believe is Christianity. These days we are all believers in democracy and it is easy to accept the view that Christian doctrine is to be defined by the will of the people in the Christian church. But this is false. As P. T. Forsyth put it, "this Revelation, constituent as it is of the Church, is the one thing that is withdrawn from its vote; because a Church would unchurch itself that voted against it."[8] There is a core of revelation by which we must abide. If we forsake it what is left is not Christianity.

There are some who see in comparative religion a key that will unlock all religious mysteries. There are certain ideas common to man which crystallise out in different ways in different parts of the world. It is such ideas that explain Christianity, they hold, just as they explain other religions. This denial of the heart of the Christian faith (and for that matter all other religions) must be firmly rejected. What is left after this kind of examination may be interesting and it may be explicable. But it is not Christianity.

There are Christian distinctives which must be maintained and without them we do not have Christianity. The primordial revelation is important. Forsyth asks his readers whether they would be prepared to let the property of their church go without a struggle if the majority voted to become theoretical anarchists "even if they were the sweetest-spirited men that ever stole a march or threw a bomb".[9] There are some things that make Christianity Christianity. Do away with them and you have a new religion. It is easier to be sympathetic to men who recognise this and dedicate themselves to the overthrow of Christianity and its replacement by say, some form of humanism, than to those who jettison the Christian distinctives while maintaining that they hold the Christian faith.

A church differs from a democracy. In a democracy there is no authority but that which arises from within, the will of the people. In a church there is no authority but that which comes from outside, the will of God. Democracy is effective when the people are energetic and help themselves, the church when God acts and redeems men. The essential thing is the indwelling of the Christ who lived and died and rose and ascended in his great work for men's salvation. It is only as it remains firmly committed to such basic teachings that the church is the church. When it departs from the great truths in the primordial revelation it has become something other than the church.

This is not to say that the ideal church is one set and rigid in all its ways. There must be flexibility. The church must adapt to new challenges and be ready to accept new ideas. But this adaptability and readiness to accept new truth must always be within the framework of a firm acceptance of the fundamental revelation. Otherwise what we have now may change again tomorrow and be something else again the day after. There is continuity as well as change in the authentic Christian church.

Perhaps an Australian can find an illustration in the Australian Constitution. This established the framework within which Australian democracy works. Any law, for example, passed by a State Parliament or by the Federal Parliament itself which conflicts with this Constitution may be declared unconstitutional by the courts. Any such law then becomes inoperative. This does not mean that Australians are bound to live in all respects as in the days when the constitution was adopted. There has been development and life and growth. Now and then an amendment to the constitution is approved. Changes may take place but the constitution is the normative authority. Whatever does not accord with it cannot be regarded as part of Australian democracy. Most of the peoples of the world, it is true, have no particular interest in this document. They prefer to live under other systems. But this does not alter the fact that if we are to find out what Australian democracy means it is to this document that we must make our appeal.

The parallel with the Bible is far from complete. I am not

suggesting that the Christian church is just as much at liberty to amend the Bible as the Australian electorate is to amend its constitution. All that I am saying is that the constitution illustrates the way a document may be normative for a particular group. What is authentically Christian is to be determined, not by what those who profess themselves Christian hold at a given point in time, but by what the Bible says. Other people may not accept it as authoritative. That is beside the point. For Christians it is this and nothing else that leads them to their final authority.

The Clarity of the Bible

One way of insisting on the decisive place of tradition or of the church is to point to the difficulties in the Bible and insist that there is need of an authoritative interpreter. We cannot understand the Bible without the help of the church is the way the reasoning runs. But it may be doubted whether the Bible is really so difficult. I do not mean there are no problems. Of course there are. Some parts of the Bible are very difficult indeed. No man, and for that matter, no church, would claim to be able to interpret everything in Scripture. And almost any passage in the Bible can be illuminated by the observations competent scholars make about it. There is much that the earnest student working with his own limited resources and insights cannot fathom. Christians can help one another, and where the church has a teaching function it can help also.

But we do not need somebody to tell us what the main lines of biblical teaching are. We are not so delivered over into the hands of the experts that we cannot speak about the Bible and its teaching without a professorial or ecclesiastical opinion to back us up. The ethical monotheism of the Old Testament is plain for all to see, as is the incarnation in the New. The centrality of the death and resurrection of Jesus are unmistakable and so is salvation by God's grace. We could go on. Through the centuries millions of ordinary men have read the Bible just as it is, without expert guidance, and have heard God speaking to them. The ordinary man can still read the Bible and understand enough of it to serve his purpose as he seeks to live for God. I am reminded of some wise words of a group of Dutch theologians. They speak of the conversation going on between the churches and proceed to what they call "the rules of the game". They begin,

In the first place, we must not think that the Bible is so difficult or mysterious that everyone must elucidate it or feel it in his own particular way. The conversation would then run into the quicksand of an uncommitted exchange of personal opinions. No, we must start from the fact that the things which the Bible has to say to us stand out clearly and squarely.[10]

In similar vein one of the Homilies issued by the Church of England during the Reformation period has to do with the reading of Scripture. It says among other things, "the humble man may search any truth boldly in the Scripture without any danger of error." The important word here is "humble". The Homily does not mean that a man cannot go astray with the Bible in his hand. He can. But he will not go into error if he reads it humbly, i.e., with a readiness to listen quietly to what God is saying and without reading his own ideas into it. I would not want to put it in quite that way myself. It sounds suspiciously like a readiness to underwrite the deliverance from error of every humble Bible reader. I guess the difficult thing is to find a man who is really "humble" in the sense the Homily means. But certainly there is a good deal in the point being made. That is to say the most fruitful source of error is not the Bible, but the things men read into the Bible. The Homily goes on to say, "those things in the Scripture that be plain to understand and necessary for salvation, every man's duty is to learn them, to print them in memory, and effectually to exercise them; and, as for the dark mysteries, to be contented to be ignorant in them until such time as it shall please God to open those things unto him".

This is not a popular opinion today, when it is widely held that one can prove anything out of the Bible. It is pointed out that those who agree on accepting the Bible do not by any manner of means agree. Even fundamentalist sects differ among themselves as to what the Bible teaches. There is certainly something in this. Sometimes the diversity goes back to a diversity within the Bible. It would be a mistake to say that the Bible teaches a monochrome kind of Christianity such that everyone who takes the Bible seriously must come out with exactly the same results. God made men different and while he did not make as many Christianities as men it is quite plain that the Bible can lead to different results even among those who take it with full seriousness. For example, there are some

Christians who accept infant baptism and others who think there must be a credible profession of faith on the part of the candidate before baptism may properly be administered. I do not think that either of these points of view is set forth in Scripture. But there are teachings about baptism which can lead to one or the other position. This kind of diversity is surely legitimate. But it is not the same as the diversity that results when men take up positions that cannot be substantiated from the Bible.

And there are limits to the diversity that bases itself on Scripture. Not everything that claims to be Christian can justify itself from the ancient records. It may be doubted whether some things that are put out under the heading "The Teaching of the Bible" are in fact just that. Often there is eisegesis as well as exegesis. What a man reads into the Bible is not fairly described as the teaching of Scripture.

We should also bear in mind that there is unity as well as diversity. Right round the world and across the denominational barriers there is an impressive measure of agreement among those who take the Bible as their authority. While I do not want to minimise the differences, yet the really striking differences are those which arise when people do not take the Bible alone as their final authority. Where more deference is paid to tradition (as in the Catholic section of the church) or to the consecrated reason (the liberals) there are significant differences from those who accept the Bible alone. But the measure of agreement among those who concentrate on the Bible is significant.

This does not mean, as some Protestants have held, that tradition should be ignored and the Bible only need be consulted. If we agree that tradition is not to be given a place comparable to that of Scripture it does not follow that we can ignore tradition. The Bible is read in the fellowship of the church. Whether we like it or not we are always influenced by the traditions of that section of the church in which we read it. When tradition becomes dead and mechanical and when it usurps the place that belongs to Scripture we must reject it. We must bear in mind our Lord's teaching about those who made void the word of God through their tradition (Mark 7: 13). This is just as possible for modern Christendom as it was for ancient Judah. But we cannot cut ourselves off from the community of faith when we read the Bible. Most Christians accept doctrines like the Trinity or those set forth in the historic creeds, doctrines formulated by the church, and we cannot read the Bible as though we were indifferent to them.

This does not mean that we give the community the supreme place. Some have said that since the church was there before the Bible the church has an inherent authority that surpasses that of the Bible. But this does not follow. In any case it misrepresents the situation for there never was a time when the church existed without a Bible. For Christopher Evans this is a distinctive of Christianity: "Christianity is unique among the great religions in being born with a Bible in its cradle. This was entirely peculiar."[11] But it happened. For Jesus and the early Christians the Bible was our Old Testament. We do not know in what regard the Epistles and the Gospels were held when they first appeared, but there is no doubting that the Old Testament was always revered by the Christians as sacred Scripture, nor that in due time the writings of the New Testament came to be regarded in the same light. By the time 2 Peter was written the Pauline Epistles were regarded as Scripture (2 Pet. 3 : 15f.). It was not so very long before a similar attitude was held towards most of the New Testament. From the very first the Christians were in the habit of appealing to their Bible. It is not too much to say that the church was established on the basis of the revelation it received, partly in the words of the Old Testament and partly in the life and teaching of Jesus. The first generation of believers could pass on to the second its personal reminiscences of Jesus, but from then on Christians have been dependent on the written record.

The Canon

Sometimes still the catch cry is raised, "The church gave us the Bible," with the implication that since the Bible is the product of the church's life the church is always at liberty to modify or replace its teachings. This is something more than the viewpoint we have just examined. There the thought was simply that the church preceded the Bible and was independent of it. Here the idea rather is that the church originated the Bible. This may be put in the form that all the people who wrote the books of the Bible were members of the church, so that the Bible should be regarded as a product of the church's life. It is the abounding life of the church that is primary. The Bible is no more than one expression of that life. Or the same essential point of view may be expressed by saying that at a time when various books circulated among the Christians it was the church that decided which should be included in the canon. Since the church had the authority to select it is always at liberty to think again about its selection. On this view the church could decide that the teaching of some book of the Bible is no longer acceptable. Or it could add some other book to the canon.

To this a number of things might be said. Firstly let us notice that it is not easy to see what meaning is to be given to "the church" in this connection. To be of any value the whole church should be brought into the process and it is not at all obvious how this could be done. Of course it might be possible to obtain the opinions of bishops or moderators or synods, but do any or all of these comprise the church? The contention points to a process that it is not at all easy to see happening.

But in any case it rests on a misconception, or rather on a number of misconceptions, of how the Bible came to the church. We have already noticed that the church was never without a Bible. In that sense it is simply not true to say that the church gave us the Bible. Rather, the church was the product of the Bible or at any rate of that part of the Bible that it already had.

We should also be clear that the New Testament did not originate in any official or formal manner from the church. Indeed we can scarcely say more than that the writers of the New Testament books were church members. Is there any meaningful sense in which we can say that the church at Corinth produced the Corinthian Epistles? Or that the church anywhere else commissioned them? It is plain that, while the life of the church in that city was not without its importance as the occasion for those letters, they come to us as the inspired product of the great apostle, not as the product of the church.

It is also worth noting that chronological priority does not mean much. The ministry of John the Baptist preceded that of our Lord and in a very real sense the ministry of Jesus rested on that of his predecessor. But we cannot argue from this that the authority of the Baptist exceeds that of Jesus. That the church existed before the New Testament has nothing to do with the relative authorities of the two. That must be decided on other grounds.

Invalid, too, is the position of those who relegate the formation of the canon to the level of a human judgment. Thus G. D. Yarnold holds that:

The assertion that the scriptures contain the Word of God to man is not a plain factual statement. . . . This principle expresses *human judgment* upon scripture. And it is important to realise that the alternative fundamentalist view, which exalts the scriptures to the status of an unquestioned absolute, is none the less a human judgement upon them. Liberal and fundamentalist are logically in the same position.[12]

He further says that the church's recognition of the canon is "essentially a human judgement, even though a corporate one."[13] But this is to overlook a number of points. To begin with, the claim of so many writers of Scripture, "Thus saith the Lord" is ignored. This claim may perhaps in the end be modified or rejected, but there is no justification for overlooking it and then saying that we are dealing with a human judgment. That is not the way it looks to those who take the biblical writers seriously. If God has indeed spoken, then the writer is not recording a human judgment. Moreover the suggestion that the church is registering "essentially a human judgement" in its recognition of the canon overlooks the fact that there has to be something to recognise. Christians have always held, not that the church holds certain books to be inspired, but that those books are inspired. The church's assent is an assent to a reality, a reality that existed and necessarily existed before the assent could be given.

Moreover the church's place in fixing the canon should not be exaggerated. The process of canonisation does not mean that any synod ever promulgated a canon reading, "This Council hereby makes this or that book canonical." Always such a decree is explanatory and declaratory. Some of the faithful have been perplexed. They have found some people accepting say, 1 Clement, and reading it in the services of worship and others refusing to accept, say, 2 and 3 John. What books *should* a Christian accept? It is all so perplexing.

So the Council or the Synod issues a list for the guidance of the puzzled faithful. But the important point is that it is always a list of books already recognised as canonical. The Council says in effect, "These are the books that the church has always accepted." It never says, "Here is a new and valuable book. Our experts have read it and like it. We decree that from now on it will form part of sacred scripture." Canonisation does not mean taking a book hitherto unrecognised and elevating it into the Bible. It is simply the recognition of an existing situation.

It is a clarification of the position by those who are best in a position to know.

It has been well said that the Bible is not so much an authorised collection of books as a collection of authorised books, of books which already have authority. It is in fact truer to say that the Bible selected itself than that the church selected the Bible. The thing that makes a book canonical is what the Holy Spirit has done in causing it to be written as it is. The church can do no more than recognise what the Spirit has done. It is the Spirit that makes canonicity. Bruce Vawter has a high regard for the place of the church, but he can say, "While the Christian does accept the inspired character of the OT (and the NT as well) on the basis of the Church's word concerning it, still it is not that word or teaching that constitutes it sacred but merely discerns it."[14]

We must distinguish between canonicity and the reasons men gave for regarding a book as canonical. It is true that Synods and Councils put forward tests such as age, authorship, helpfulness and the like. But in the end it was not so much that the church gave us the books as that God gave the books to the church. Theoretically God might have guided the church to commission people to write the books she needed. But that is not how the books in fact came to be written. Holy men of God wrote them as they were guided by God to write them. The Bible represents God's gift to his church as the embodiment of his revelation.

The Bible in the Beginning

Confusion is sometimes caused by statements that it took centuries for the church to determine the canon. The implication is that for hundreds of years the church did not know what books were in the Bible and still managed quite well. There is thus no need for us to worry overmuch about the Bible. We, too, could get along without it. But this is to ignore the facts.

In the first place, as we have already noticed, from the beginning the church had a Bible. The Old Testament was always in its hands. And the content of the Old Testament was not a matter for dispute. We do not know exactly how and when the Old Testament canon was fixed, but it seems clear that by New Testament times our present Old Testament was generally accepted just as it is. It is sometimes said that the Old Testament canon was not settled until the Synod of Jamnia, c. A.D. 90, but this is far too confident. Little is known about what took place at Jamnia, but to speak of "the Synod (or Council) of Jamnia" as though it were a definite assembly on a given date is to go beyond our knowledge. After the Romans had taken Jerusalem in A.D. 70 R. Johanan b. Zakkai secured permission to establish a school at Jamnia (also called Jabneh), a town on the coastal plain.[15] Scholars gathered round him and the place became an important centre for Jewish culture. With the cessation of Temple worship and all that went with it a great number of matters had to be determined. The scholars at Jamnia lacked the formal authority of the Sanhedrin but in the altered circumstances their pronouncements carried a lot of weight.

Among the subjects they discussed at some time was the canon. As far as our information goes there never was serious discussion as to whether a given book should be *included* in the canon (though some attention was given to Ecclesiasticus). The rabbis were dealing with a definite, known canon and they aired scholarly doubts about the legitimacy of some of the books on the list, notably Ecclesiastes and the Song of Songs. This had been a matter of discussion between the schools of Hillel and Shammai in the time of Jesus and the Mishnah records a decision on the day when R. Eleazar b. Azariah was installed as head of the college (which happened during the Jamnia period) that both are canonical (*Yadaim* 3: 5).

It is probably this kind of thing that leads to the idea that the Jewish canon was still in a state of flux. But this is to misread the situation. There is no evidence of serious discussion as to what books should or should not be in the canon. Rather these are scholarly debates on the objections sometimes raised to a few of the books and in every case the objections were met to the satisfaction of the rabbis and the case against dismissed. As Aage Bentzen puts it, the discussions at Jamnia "have not so much dealt with acceptance of certain writings into the Canon, but rather with their *right to remain there*. . . . If we study the discussions in the *Mishna* and the *Talmud* we see that it is always *presupposed that the disputed books are canonical*. . . . The synod of the rabbis tries to account for the right of the *books* to be parts of the *Book*."[16] The men of Jamnia raised scholarly points like the problem of how to reconcile parts of Ezekiel (especially the provisions for worship in chs. 40-48) with the Mosaic laws, whether Proverbs should be excluded from the canon on the grounds that there is a contradiction between

26: 4 and 26: 5, and the like. But there is no evidence that this group of scholars did more than re-affirm an already existing canon and one which is independently corroborated by Josephus.[17] While discussions went on among the learned there is no real reason for doubting that by New Testament times the Old Testament canon was fixed. Jesus and the apostles accepted the Old Testament as the Jews had it at that time and as we have it now. The church had no occasion to pronounce on this and in fact never did.

As for the books we call the Apocrypha, there is no evidence that they were regarded as authoritative. One of them, Ecclesiasticus, is explicitly said not to be canonical,[18] and while there seem to be no pronouncements on the others there is no doubt that they were regarded in the same way. They were edifying, but not authoritative. They are not in the Hebrew Old Testament (though some of them may have been written in Hebrew), but appear only in the Greek version. And for Christians the matter appears to be settled by the fact that they are not appealed to as authoritative anywhere in the New Testament. We may read them with profit still, but we do not appeal to them to establish doctrine.

It is true that we do not get an authoritative list giving exactly our New Testament books, no more and no less, until we come to the Festal Letter of Athanasius in A.D. 367. But that should not blind us to the fact that from early days there was little doubt about the greater part of our New Testament. The four Gospels and none other were accepted, and so were Acts, the Pauline Epistles, 1 Peter, 1 John and usually the Revelation. Hesitation was felt about Hebrews and in some quarters about Revelation. I do not wish to over-simplify, but it does seem that for the most part discussion centred on the smaller books. We may well feel that there would have been loss had any been finally excluded. But no great doctrine of the Christian faith hung on the issue. The characteristic Christian position was made amply clear in the books about which there was no doubt from quite early days.

And the church clung tenaciously to those books. It is true that occasionally men like Marcion or Montanus appeared with other ideas and tried to shorten or extend the canon. But they were emphatically rejected. What they were trying to do was seen as monstrous. Herman Ridderbos brings out something of what was involved when he says: "This infringement upon what the Church acknowledged as incontestable apostolic

depository was something that made it stagger on its founda-
tions."[19] The canon was fundamental.

From the beginning the books of the New Testament were
normally seen as different from all others. Long ago Westcott
pointed out that the successors of the apostles seem to have
perceived this intuitively:

> they had certainly an indistinct perception that their work
> was essentially different from that of their predecessors. . . .
> Without having any exact sense of the completeness of the
> Christian Scriptures, they still drew a line between them and
> their own writings. As if by some providential instinct, each
> one of those teachers who stood nearest to the writers of the
> New Testament contrasted his writings with theirs, and
> definitely placed himself on a lower level.[20]

This is contrary to what might have been expected. In those
first days we would not have anticipated that there would have
been a sharp distinction between the writings now regarded as
canonical and other Christian writings. But the distinction was
in fact drawn. The writers nearest to the New Testament
definitely put themselves on a lower level. In other words, from
the very first it has been clear to the church that the writings
of church members generally are not to be regarded as
authoritative in the way the Bible is.[21] This is not an official
judgment on the canon but a striking testimony to the power of
the canonical Scriptures. They have the stamp of God on them.
Robert McAfee Brown can say, "The very fact that the canon
was established is the best evidence that the early Church was
determined to distinguish between the apostolic tradition and
all later tradition, and to insist that the former be the norm for
the latter."[22]

It is important to be clear that the Bible has always occupied
a central place in the Christian understanding of things. As
Karl Barth once put it, "At bottom, the Church is in the world
only with a book in its hands. . . . And if we are asked, What
have you to say? we can only answer, Here something has been
said and what is said we want to hear."[23]

The Authoritative Revelation

The decisive revelation, the authoritative deposit of the
Christian faith, is in the Bible and the Bible only. Other books

may be helpful, but that does not mean that they share the Bible's authority. Sometimes Scriptural books are compared with other books to the disparagement of the Scriptural writings, as in C. H. Dodd's preference for Ecclesiasticus over Esther.[24] It is important to be clear that books are included in the Bible not because they appeal to us more than do other books, nor even because they are more helpful to us than other books (though for most Christians this is in fact the case). They are included because these are the books that God has given his people to provide the authoritative guidance for their faith. God may well inspire other authors, including modern writers, to write edifying books. But the fact that they are edifying does not make them authoritative in the biblical sense. The Bible is unique. Here we have the record of "the faith which was once for all delivered to the saints" (Jude 3).

This arises out of the very nature of the Christian faith. This is not simply a collection of timeless truths, a quintessence of the wisdom of the ages. Were that so then the canon might well be open more or less permanently, for with the advance of knowledge who would dare to say that the Holy Spirit might not inspire some further servant of God to add to the previous truths already enshrined in Holy Writ?

But the Christian faith is the message of what God has done for our salvation. The essential Christian message is the good news of what God has done in Christ. Once that action has been performed there is no adding to it. The Bible is the book that bears the definitive witness to what God has done. Once that witness has been borne there is no adding to it, or, for that matter, subtracting from it. The whole Bible is involved. The Old Testament concentrates on the mighty acts of God in Israel's history, but treats them as events of theological significance that point forward. This is not simply a matter of prophecies that would be fulfilled in the coming of Jesus (though that is part of the picture). It is a laying down of certain important theological truths about the nature of God and of man, about the relationship of God to man, about the nature of life and of sin, and about the way sin may be forgiven. All this prepares the way for the New Testament, with its message in the Gospels of the Son of God come for man's salvation, in the Acts of the way the first Christian preachers went forth with the message of salvation, and in the Epistles with the reflections of the writers on the meaning of what God had done for man.

The Closed Canon

The message thus given is definitive and there is no need and no place for an addition to the canon. John Bright argues that we would suffer loss if one or other of the smaller books of the Bible were to be lost, and that we would have a gain that we would prize highly if in some new Qumran we were to find the writings of another authentic minor prophet or a new apostolic epistle. But this would not affect the total picture of the theology of the Bible and it is this that matters. "It is through its theology that the Bible speaks its authoritative word."[25] The canon is wide enough to determine the basic theology of the gospel and it is this that counts. Once it is established there is no point in any further addition. Moreover, more than prophetic or apostolic authorship is involved in canonicity. Usage through the centuries, for example, is important. Doubtless Christians will continue to find books that are edifying and stimulating. But the closed canon points to a truth of permanent importance. God has acted to bring men salvation and he has not left himself without adequate witness to what he has done. The Bible is not a compendium of religious knowledge, a book in which we might expect to find an answer to all our religious questions. It is the sufficient witness to what God has done for our salvation.

It is this that sets the Bible apart from all other literature. And it is this that means that we must not set the church (or anything else) above the Bible. Nothing can replace the authentic deposit of Christian truth. Indeed so far from the church being superior to the Bible the church must always submit itself to the Bible and test its teaching against the Bible. From time to time the church has found itself in need of reformation and doubtless the situation will recur. On what principle is the church to reform itself? Surely on none other than that of faithfulness to the Scripture. It is the Bible that gives the authentic Christian message. When the church can demonstrate that it is faithfully proclaiming that message it can claim to be on the right track. When it cannot, it is in need of reform. This does not mean that the church is limited, say in matters of community organisation, to the patterns of the first century. But it does mean that the teaching of the New Testament is decisive, that what we do must accord with the great principles there set forth.

This must be maintained in the face of that modern radical movement which ascribes no special significance to the Bible.

This presupposes that man is in a position of and by himself to lay it down how and when God will make his revelation. Modern man determines what revelation is and to what he will submit as authoritative. It would seem that he decides that the Bible is not particularly authoritative and therefore it is not particularly authoritative. But it may be asked whether there is any reason why modern man should be in this way the measure of things.

James Barr gives attention to the contention of the modern biblical theology movement that the Bible is the record of the acts of God and he finds it defective. He thinks that there is a good deal in the Bible that cannot be regarded as "reportage of events".[26] Above all this includes "the various theologies of the writers".[27] He apparently finds the problem here that in any given case it has not been shown that the theology of the writer is the *necessary* interpretation of the facts rather than no more than one of a number of possible interpretations.

A Priori Reasoning

But this is again to lay down in advance what God must do. If he is to produce a Bible he must do it in such and such a way. I find this kind of *a priori* reasoning unsatisfactory. I do not know what are the conditions for bringing about the writings of a Bible. I do not know how God could cause a man to write an authoritative document. I do not see why he should not cause men to include things other than the reportage of events in his Bible if he so wished. Nor do I see why he should not make use of the theology or theologies of the writers if his purpose could be accomplished in that way. I do not find it a problem that the theology of a given writer is not the one necessary interpretation. On the contrary I do not see how any sort of Bible could be produced without each of the writers opting for one out of several possible interpretations. Such an event, for example, as the crucifixion would certainly be interpreted differently by different observers. It is hard to see how Caiaphas could possibly have interpreted it in the same way as did Pilate or Peter or Paul or one of the Evangelists. But I do not see how that prevents an account from contributing to God's revelation. I would not want to lay it down that unless there is a necessary interpretation of this event God could not cause a record of it to be included in the Bible. I see no reason why he should not cause more than one account to be recorded, and, for that matter, more than one interpretation. I simply do not know enough about God to be dogmatic. It seems to me much better to ask what God has done than to reject in advance the possibility that he might do anything because I do not see how he could do it.

Another variant of the *a priori* approach is provided by D. E. Nineham. He says of "many theologians" that they "want each passage to have a meaning because they want the Bible as a whole to have a meaning".[28] It may well be that there are theologians like this. But it might have been better for Nineham to have given attention to those who lack the presupposition of what he speaks. It would be at least equally true (and perhaps more meaningful) to say that "many theologians" find meaning in individual passages of the Bible because they have found the Bible as a whole to have meaning. So with Nineham's "Granted the assumption, common to (Luther) and his opponents, that some single external and objective criterion of doctrine was necessary. . . ."[29] Whatever be the case with Luther and his enemies there are many today who do not make the assumption and who yet find the Bible authoritative. They ask, not "What must God do?" but "What has God done?"

It is amusing that Nineham seems to be guilty of exactly the fault he finds in others. Thus he complains that Barth "does not consider the possibility—which is precisely the question at issue—that God does not *wish* His self-revelation to 'possess the character of an authority irremovably confronting the Church'."[30] But Nineham does not consider the possibility that God *does* wish this. It is this *a priori* approach, that God could not conceivably behave other than in a way a modern scholar would approve, that many find so unsatisfactory. Would it not be better to look at the Bible and ask what God in fact has done?

NOTES

1. John Macquarrie, *Principles of Christian Theology* (London: 1966), p. 7.
2. *Ibid.*, p. 8.
3. Jerome, *Dial.adv.Lucif.*, 19.
4. Macquarrie, *Principles of Christian Theology*, p. 83.

5. Christopher Evans, *S.P.C.K. Theological Collections*, no. 1 (London: 1960), p. 75.
   He goes on to notice a corresponding Roman Catholic horror; "it is difficult to exaggerate the horror of the Catholic at the replacement of the beloved communion of saints, across the world and down the ages, living and departed, by what seems to him a desert stretching between the death of the last apostle to write in the Scriptures and the second coming of the Lord, and ourselves left to find our way in the desert only by the reading and preaching of the word" (*ibid.*, p. 76).
6. Karl Hermann Schelkle, Ludwig Klein ed., *The Bible in a New Age* (London: 1965), p. 143.
7. Christopher Evans, *S.P.C.K. Theological Collections*, p. 78.
8. P. T. Forsyth, *The Principle of Authority* (London: 1952), p. 230.
9. *Ibid.*, p. 233.
10. *The Bible Speaks Again* (London: 1969), p. 198.
11. Christopher Evans, *Is "Holy Scripture" Christian?* (London: 1971) p. 2.
12. G. D. Yarnold, *By What Authority?* (London: 1964), p. 26 (Yarnold's italics).
13. *Ibid.*, p. 28.
14. Bruce Vawter, *Biblical Inspiration* (London: 1972), pp. 160f.
15. Talmud, *Gittin*, 56b.
16. Aage Bentzen, *Introduction to the Old Testament* (Copenhagen: 1948), Vol. 1, p. 31. Cf. R. K. Harrison, "The conversations that took place were strictly academic, and in consequence it is very questionable if the doubts that they raised in connection with certain compositions actually represented the general attitude of the populace as a whole to any significant extent. Certainly Ezekiel, to mention but one topic of dispute, must have been accepted as Scripture long before the rabbis of Jamnia undertook to examine its status. It ought to be concluded, therefore, that no formal pronouncement as to the limits of the Old Testament canon was ever made in rabbinic circles at Jamnia" (*Introduction to the Old Testament* (Grand Rapids: 1969), pp. 278f.). Similarly F. F. Bruce can say, "The books which they decided to acknowledge as canonical were already generally accepted, although questions had been raised about them. Those which they refused to admit had never been included. They did not expel from the canon any book which had previously been admitted. 'The Council of Jamnia', as J. S. Wright puts it, 'was the confirming of public opinion, not the forming of it' " (*The Books and the Parchments* (London: 1963), p. 98).
17. *Contra Apion*, 1, 8 (Loeb edn., 1, 38).
18. See G. F. Moore, *Judaism* (Harvard: 1958), Vol. 1, p. 86. The same passage condemns "the gospel" and the books of the sectarians, which most agree at least includes the writings of the Christians.
19. Herman Ridderbos, in Carl F. H. Henry ed., *Revelation and the Bible* (London: 1959), p. 199.
20. B. F. Westcott, *A General Survey of the History of the Canon of the New Testament* (Cambridge and London: 1875), p. 56.
21. See for example, the passages cited on pp. 63ff., above.
22. Robert McAfee Brown. Cited in Dewey M. Beegle, *Scripture, Tradition, and Infallibility* (Grand Rapids: 1973), p. 119.
23. Karl Barth, *God in Action* (Edinburgh: 1937), pp. 107f.
24. C. H. Dodd, *The Authority of the Bible* (London: 1947), p. 161.

25. John Bright, *The Authority of the Old Testament* (Nashville: 1967), p. 158.
26. James Barr, *The Bible in the Modern World* (London: 1973), p. 85.
27. *Ibid.*
28. D. E. Nineham, *Bulletin of the John Rylands Library*, Vol. 52 (1969), p. 128.
29. *Ibid.*, p. 183.
30. *Ibid.*, p. 197.

CHAPTER 5

A Word from God

IT WAS A VIRTUE of old-fashioned fundamentalism that it gave its adherents an unquestioned word from God. When the fundamentalist sat (or sits; the breed survives) before his Bible he was secure in the knowledge that as he read those sacred pages he would receive a message from God. These days he is often accused of "bibliolatry", the worship of a book. In all fairness this charge ought to be dropped. It may well be that any fundamentalist pays more respect to the words of the Bible taken in their most literal meaning than his critical brother would like. But that does not mean that he worships the book. I have never known a fundamentalist against whom the charge would lie fairly. Every one of them I have known or whose writings I have read regards the Bible as the means of hearing God's voice. It is God he seeks, not the book. What marks him out is his confidence that through the Bible God will in sure and certain truth speak to him.

Critical scholarship seems by and large to have lost this confidence. The writer to the Hebrews could affirm that in former days God "spoke" through the prophets and more recently that "he has spoken" in the Son (Heb. 1: 1f.). But modern scholarship has mostly lost this. In discarding fundamentalist literalism it has discarded also the word from God, a classical case of throwing out the baby with the bathwater. J. V. Langmead Casserley comments bitingly, "We are confronted with the paradox of a way of studying the word of God out of which no word of God ever seems to come."[1] Paul S. Minear points out that for many church members "heaven is silent and God does not speak".[2] That such esti-

mates are not exaggerated could be readily substantiated
by appeal to modern writers. It will suffice to cite a well-
known dictum of William Temple, "no single sentence can
be quoted as having the authority of an authentic utterance
of the All-Holy God."[3] Not one.

Scholars like Casserley and Minear readily concede the
gains made by the modern critical approach. It has increased
our understanding of the Bible immensely. It has delivered
us from slavish adherence to impossible literalistic interpretations of the Bible. But the question they raise is whether
these benefits have been purchased at too great a cost. It is
possible to read quite long books from modern biblical
scholars, books avowedly written about the Bible, and yet
finish with nothing more than a mass of information about
ancient literature. We could do as well with Homer or Virgil.
Is this the way to study the Bible?

Casserley points out that this failure to find a word from
God is not accidental, but arises from the very nature of the
critical method. He speaks of

> certain characteristic philosophical postulates and affilia-
> tions which render it impossible for a man conscientiously
> adhering to the conventions and methodological rules of
> self-consciously modern history quite to come to grips with
> some of the basic biblical themes. In other words, we
> have to consider not what modern biblical criticism fails
> to do, so to speak, accidentally, but what it cannot do
> essentially, because it is the kind of "blunt" instrument that
> it is.[4]

Critical scholars seem usually to have a quite uncritical
reverence for their critical method. They assume that, properly
used, it cannot but bring us to the truth. Each recognises
with becoming humility that he himself has not yet reached
final conclusions, but this humility does not extend to his
view of the method. This is accepted as the only satisfactory
way of studying the Bible today. The thought that there may
be a basic flaw in the method seems never to be given serious
consideration. This is illustrated by the fact that, though
Casserley's book appeared in 1965 very few seem to have
taken any notice of this section of it. Apparently it seems to
the general run of scholars so incredible that Casserley should
be right that it is not even worth examining his arguments.

And they keep turning out their studies of the word of God from which no sure word of God ever comes.

Brevard S. Childs complains of the exegesis that results from the modern approach. The historico-critical method can give us a good deal of information about the original meaning of the passage, but Childs does not see it as following that "the original function is alone normative".[5] The Bible has a meaning for us now and it is the important task of the exegete to tell us what that meaning is. He complains of the modern idea of what constitutes a commentary and refers to one on 1 Kings 13 which "provides detailed information on the different kinds of trees in Palestine, the variety of lions, and the grave furniture of Early Bronze family tombs". He proceeds, "Although it would not be fair to blame the critical method for the author's tone-deafness to theological issues, the method is at fault in attributing such high priority to questions that are of such tangential importance to the story's own perspective."[6]

Childs see the older commentators as being at pains to relate the passage with which they are dealing to its context in canonical Scripture, a concern almost totally absent from modern works. But we ought never to try to interpret a biblical passage without being conscious of its function as part of a whole, the Bible. The Old Testament looks on to the New, the New back to the Old. Neither can be ignored. In a final salvo Childs complains of

> a type of critical training that has the effect of closing the Biblical student to all but a few questions. When our seminary-trained pastors find Augustine incomprehensible, Luther verbose, and Calvin dull, then obviously the problem lies with the reader and his theological education and not with the old masters.[7]

The Dutch scholars who produced the book *The Bible Speaks Again* make the same essential point. They ask, "should (the Bible) not be questioned differently from the way in which the critical-historical method does it?" and proceed,

> Thus it comes about that, in spite of the probing researches of the scientists, one often has the impression that their analyses and their researchers have missed the real contents of the Bible. To put it in a somewhat homely image: the

critical scientific approach to the Bible sometimes makes one think of trying to eat soup with a fork. What is offered in the many commentaries concerning the authenticity, the reality, the dependence on others' sources, and so on, is not so much wrong as beside the point. The same rationalism which we thought we had seen at work in orthodox theology has, in various guises, also affected the scientific research of the Bible, making it so scanty, so unfruitful, seemingly so negative, that congregations have been shocked, while the theologians and preachers often see no other way than to ignore the results of such research, or to fight against it from a negative standpoint.[8]

They disavow any intention of pulling up too quickly "all the weeds of the new 'liberalism' ", for they find some truth there. But they are sure that theologians like Bultmann, John Robinson and van Buren are not leading us forward. Indeed they say of them: "they cannot become really up-to-date, concrete and 'with it'. They are following modern man (without catching up with him), rather than going ahead of him."[9]

Such a suspicion is surely not confined to the Dutch theologians. Too many modern radical scholars are not leading us to a better way of finding the word from God for our day and generation. Rather they are caught up with the niceties of the problems scholarship discerns. The result can be fascinating. But it is not of much help to men seeking a word from God. The Dutchmen make the further important point that many scholars who complain about the way conservatives lag behind are themselves not in fact among the leaders in modern thought. The drawback to allowing the modern world to dictate the terms is that one must always be just that bit behind the modern world.

Revelation
Scholarship does not seem to take revelation seriously enough. In handling the biblical documents it prefers to proceed along lines that would be congenial to the atheist or the agnostic. For the atheist there is no question of revelation. There is no God and there can be no revelation. The agnostic holds that if there is a God he is unable to reveal himself, or at least never does reveal himself in such a way as to carry conviction. Such a god makes no difference to anybody. He may safely be ignored.

Too many biblical scholars approach the Bible as though they were atheists or agnostics, or at best deists, holding to the existence of a god who is absent from the world or at least from the writing of the Bible. Whatever they may say in theory about the inspiration of Holy Writ, in practice they treat it as another human document. Not infrequently they pride themselves on doing just this. They suggest that it is necessary to treat the biblical records in the same way as we treat other ancient documents if we are to see them as they are. But this is to overlook the fact that if the Bible is the record of God's revelation it is not just another ancient book.

Casserley refers to the doctrines of providence and of biblical inspiration and poses the options open to us: "The difficulty is that if these doctrines have any truth in them at all they certainly cannot be ignored in any kind of rational practice, and if they have no truth in them whatsoever, we can hardly be justified in professing any kind of Christianity."[10] But how often does a biblical scholar make any allowance for the fact that he is dealing with an inspired document?

It is the divine initiatives, the acts of God, that matter most. If God is working out a purpose in the affairs of men then nothing can compare in importance with that purpose. It will be well for us to take careful note of the words and deeds of the men in whom that purpose is most significantly set forward. But if we are to be true to the basic thought that God is at work we will not stop at those words and deeds. We will go on to ask, "What is God doing here?" and "What is God saying here?" Many recent scholars use phrases like "the God who acts". But when we ask what God has done the result is surprisingly meagre. They are loath to see any specific act as divine. The "scandal of particularity" is strong in this area. There is no great problem in discovering what those who profess to serve God have done and said. But the deeds of God and the words of God are quite another matter.

By contrast the men of the Bible frequently come out with "Thus saith the Lord" or its equivalent. And they are not backward in recognising the hand of God in unusual events in men and in nature. For them "the acts of God" was more than a pious phrase. They could and did point to specific deeds which they ascribed to God. For them God really acts. He is not simply thought to act. Modern men lack this confidence.

Casserley distinguishes between what he calls "the naked

acts" of God and his "veiled acts".[11] The naked acts represent
God's making bare his holy arm and doing works that we would
call supernatural or miraculous. His veiled acts are his "working in the hearts of men, inspiring the prophets and the saints,
or even moving the minds of men who are anything but
prophets and saints to act in a way that conforms with the
divine plan".[12] Casserley points out that if the naked acts
occurred at all we must grant that they are works of God.
There is no other explanation. But the veiled acts are such
that it is quite possible to hold that they occurred while
denying that God was involved in them.

Now it is only in these "veiled acts" that the typical modern
biblical scholar is prepared to see God at work. This has the
unfortunate effect, as Casserley notes, that his position is
always open to criticism by the opponent who declares that he
"has no need of that hypothesis". It is the "naked acts" that
openly affirm God to be God and show him to be willing to
act in the affairs of men. And this is the God of the Bible.
Paul could say of the act of God in raising Jesus from the dead,
"this was not done in a corner" (Acts 26:26). God has acted
strikingly and for the men of the Bible his deeds can be
perceived.

Experience and Reality

Some complain about what Casserley calls "biblical Kantian-
ism".[13] He points out that Kant and some other philosophers
held that we never know the real thing, the "thing in itself".
All that we know is the way we experience it. In the biblical
equivalent we are asked to believe that what we have in the
Bible is not the reality but only human experience of that
reality. For example, we do not find Jesus in the Gospels
as he was but only as the early church saw him. There is no
way of getting past the church to the real Jesus.

But this is too pessimistic. The time interval between the
life of Jesus and the composition of our Gospels is too short
for all trace of Jesus to have disappeared. It is instructive to
compare the way historians of the ancient world approach
their sources these days with that of New Testament scholars.
The latter insist that we can find out about the early church
and its ideas, not about Jesus. The former are increasingly
confident about their ability to use their sources to give genuine
information about events and characters of the day.

James M. Robinson draws our attention to a piece of

terminology which must be noted carefully if we are to use recent works on the Gospels. " 'Historical' is used in the sense of 'things in the past which have been established by objective scholarship'. Consequently the expression 'historical Jesus' comes to mean: 'What can be known of Jesus of Nazareth by means of the scientific methods of the historian'."[14] Again he says, " 'The historical Jesus' comes really to mean no more than 'the historian's Jesus'. The clear implication is that 'Jesus of Nazareth as he actually was' may be considerably more than or quite different from 'the historical Jesus'."[15]

This dependence on the work of the historian rules out as impossible any idea of a Jesus who is greater than man. The historico-critical method is a method which proceeds on the basis of a careful scrutiny of what is human. It has no tools to go beyond that. The unfortunate consequence of limiting ourselves to what can be discovered by this method is that it rules out in advance the possibility that Jesus may be an incarnation of God or at least it refrains from making any pronouncement on the possibility. This would not be so bad if it made it quite clear what it is doing and drew attention to the possibility that God was in Christ reconciling the world to himself and if it went on to say that its method left it unable to say anything one way or the other on this subject. But as it is commonly practised the historico-critical method gives the impression that when it is through everything that can be said on the subject has been said. Anything more is pious conjecture.

It is this which is leading many to affirm that the method has crippling limitations. G. E. Ladd says forthrightly, "In sum, the historical-critical method is not an adequate method to interpret the theology of the New Testament because its presuppositions limit its findings to the exclusion of the central biblical message."[16] Any method which has nothing to say about the central affirmations of the New Testament is clearly of limited value. I am not saying that the method is value-less. All serious students are indebted to it. But I am saying that we must not be hypnotised by it. There is more to Jesus than "the Jesus of history" (in Robinson's sense) and more to the Bible than an historical source book.

But there are others who see that the Christ of faith is not to be separated from the Jesus of history. Long ago Gerhard Kittel said,

The Jesus of History is valueless and unintelligible unless He be experienced and confessed by faith as the living Christ. But, if we would be true to the New Testament, we must at once reverse this judgment. The Christ of faith has no existence, is mere noise and smoke, apart from the reality of the Jesus of History. These two are utterly inseparable in the New Testament. They cannot even be thought of apart. . . . Anyone who attempts first to separate the two and then to describe only one of them, has nothing in common with the New Testament.[17]

More recently R. S. Barbour warns against the twin errors of seeing the Jesus of history as the only real Jesus (with the Christ of faith an ideal construction in our minds) and the Christ of faith as the only reality (with the Jesus of history simply an inferred figure, "the ultimately inaccessible historical reality").[18] Either distorts and oversimplifies. We need both. Barbour holds that in a right approach "we shall start by refusing to accept that the historical Jesus and the Christ of faith must necessarily be separable Gestalten at all."[19] "We can have no picture of 'the Christ of faith' in any kind of abstraction from what Jesus was."[20]

The fact that men with such divergent ideas can unite in finding the trite distinction between "the Jesus of history" and "the Christ of faith" unsatisfactory surely means something. There is a word from God available to us in the Bible which is not amenable to disclosure by the use of the critical method by itself. It is better to go along with F. V. Filson: "I work with the conviction that the only really objective method of study takes the reality of God and his working into account, and that any other point of view is loaded with presuppositions which actually, even if subtly, contain an implicit denial of the full Christian faith."[21]

There is a very sensible article by Ted Peters, "The Use of Analogy in Historical Method"[22] in which he notices the dilemma posed by Van A. Harvey: "Without the principle of analogy, it seems impossible to understand the past; if, however, one employs the principle of analogy, it seems impossible to do justice to the alleged uniqueness of Jesus Christ."[23] He goes on to show that, while there are no analogies to Jesus Christ and specifically to his resurrection, there are also no analogies which would put our information about him into the class of myth or the like: "historical research has not produced any convincing evidence that the event of Jesus' resurrection fits the model of myth, pure legend or delusion. Consequently, the use of positive analogy alone is insufficient to render the event unhistorical." He concludes, "The historian, then, must simply examine the witnesses or sources, gather the evidence, and draw a conclusion as to the most probable explanation for the experiences reported in the NT documents."[24] It is too easily assumed by those who doubt the supernatural that the Gospels can be put into some class of myth, legend or the like. Peters's point that there is no analogy along these lines is valuable. And he is surely making a valid point when he looks for "the most probable explanation" on the basis of the facts. These facts will include the claims of Jesus and the claims of Scripture, and from another direction the experience of those who through the centuries have trusted both.

On the purely historical level, then, we might reasonably expect biblical scholars to be respectful of the documents they handle. In addition there seems no reason why they should forget that they are dealing with inspired writings. This does not mean a return to narrow fundamentalism. It means that we should strive for balance. On the one hand we have writers who insist that all we need bear in mind is inspiration. This guarantees the literal truth of every word of sacred writ. On the other we have writers who treat these documents as though there was no such thing as inspiration. What is very much needed in days when the message of the Bible is so often muted is that a right balance be struck. We should not take the books of the Bible out of the realm of literature generally and put them in a glass case where no awkward questions may be asked and where we take no notice of genre, individual peculiarities and the like. But we should not forget either that God has spoken through these writings. We do them less than justice if we treat them as though we were atheists or agnostics. A balanced position requires that both the human characteristics and the divine inspiration be given due emphasis.

The Scientific Approach
One of the interesting episodes in the interpretation of the Old Testament in modern times is Julius Wellhausen's recognition of the limitations of the scientific method. He

was professor of theology at the university of Greifswald from 1872 until 1882, a period in which he wrote some important books such as *Die Komposition des Hexateuch* and the first volume of *Geschichte Israels*. But he withdrew from his post at Greifswald and became professor of Semitic languages at Halle. He wrote a letter giving his reasons:

> I became a theologian because I was interested in the scientific treatment of the Bible; it has only gradually dawned upon me that a professor of theology likewise has the practical task of preparing students for service in the Evangelical Church, and that I was not fulfilling this practical task, but rather, in spite of all reserve on my part, was incapacitating my hearers for their office.[25]

Not all agreed with Wellhausen's action, nor with his reason for acting as he did. But at least he recognised the problem we are facing. He saw that there is a way of studying the Old Testament which fails to hear a word from God in it and he recognised that, while this method has its validity, it is not the right way for a man who wishes to be a minister in the church of God. It may be that Wellhausen was too pessimistic about his method. Some have thought so and have insisted that the scientific treatment of the Bible is a necessity if a man is ever to be worth his salt as a minister and specifically as a preacher. On the other hand others have agreed with Wellhausen and admired him for courageously recognising what was happening and taking the appropriate action.

Whatever be the resolution of this problem, in my opinion Wellhausen was undoubtedly right on the main issue. It is possible to study the Old Testament in such a way that no word from God comes through; and this is not the way those who are to lead Christian congregations should study it.

Alfred Jepsen treats Wellhausen's problem with sympathy and understanding, illuminated by a profound admiration for the achievements of that great scholar. He recognises that it is possible to study the Old Testament in such a way that God's voice is not heard. He thinks that Wellhausen's isolation of Old Testament studies from theology was harmful but he adds, "A theology that was shaped by Schleiermacher, Ritschl, and Harnack could accord the Old Testament merely a historical, not a properly theological, significance."[26] He goes on to argue that "only if the Old Testament is canonical Scripture does it belong in the sphere of Christian theology. But it can only be canonical if God in some way speaks in it."[27] That is the critical point. The reason Christians continue to study the Old Testament and do not regard it simply as a piece of ancient Jewish literature is that in it they hear the God and Father of our Lord Jesus Christ. It follows that any method of studying it that does not enable them to hear the voice of God is by that very fact condemned.

Reading the Bible

All this may be relevant to James D. Smart's contention that, while biblical scholarship has made impressive advances, people are reading the Bible less. He thinks that the primary reason for this is a breakdown in communication. Biblical scholars are unaware of what is being done in departments of theology other than their own, preachers are unaware of what the scholars can tell them and congregations are unaware of what the preachers are saying.[28]

There may be something in this, for despite the wonders of modern means of communication there are some curious gaps. But may it not be that part of the reason is that the biblical scholars to whom Smart pays such generous tribute are guilty of the sin of which Langmead Casserley accuses them? So much modern biblical scholarship is learned in the extreme, but tentative or even embarrassed when it comes to hearing a word from God. Why should preachers or congregations pay attention to the Bible if they cannot hear the voice of God in it? And why should members of congregations listen to preachers if the preachers cannot bring them that word from God? Any method of studying the Bible that prevents men from hearing God is bound to result in a diminution of interest in Scripture.

Sometimes Smart seems to recognise this. Thus he notices Rudolf Kittel's recognition that the method of Old Testament scholars "seemed to be destroying the basis both for its own existence within a faculty of *Christian* theology and for the continued interest of Christian people in its findings."[29] He sees Rudolf Bultmann also as agreeing that the task of New Testament scholarship was to liberate the word of God for the church, but that New Testament scholars, for all their great achievements, "were stopping short of this essential point and thereby failing the church in its most vital function, the preaching of its gospel".[30] He notices that at various times scholars have produced devastating results and says:

> The average scholar does not appreciate how devastating his critical analysis can be to the preacher. Wilhelm Vischer, in his *The Witness of the Old Testament to Christ*, points out how the stories of the patriarchs in Genesis for thousands of years interested and instructed the generations of both Jews and Christians but in the hands of the literary critics fell silent.[31]

Again, he complains that biblical scholarship has itself contributed to a "process of alienation unintentionally in that, in its endeavour to be scientifically objective in its analysis of the literature and its reconstruction of the history and religion, it neglected the theological content of the text which alone secures its relevance for succeeding ages".[32]

Smart appears to think that the basic problem is one of communication. If only the scholars could get over to people the great things they are saying all would be well. But it seems to me that the trouble is otherwise. All too often the scholars are not passing on a clear word from God. We can hear the word of man through them, but not the word of God. And where that word does not come through the reading of the Bible is bound to decline.

"Insights"

It is not only the scientific method that prevents men from hearing the word of God. Sometimes a more sympathetic and "theological" approach may do the same. I think of some words of S. T. Coleridge, that "the words of the Bible find me in greater depths of my being; and that whatever finds me brings with it an irresistible evidence of its having proceeded from the Holy Spirit".[32] Here it is religious insight that enables the revelation to be apprehended and many have cited Coleridge's words and taken up much the same position in the sure conviction that they were holding fast to the concept of revelation.

But the trouble is that people who take up this position are apt to deny the title "revelation" to what does not "find" them. They have no criterion wherewith to tell the difference between what is authentically the voice of God and what

the result of their own human insight. The individual may be
convinced that a certain passage or a certain book is the
authentic word of God because it makes its appeal to him
deep down. But if it makes no similar appeal to his neighbour
then what is he to say? We can scarcely hold that the book
of a certain prophet is revelation for some people but not for
others. That is to make nonsense of the whole concept of
revelation and reduce it to a subjective experience. And it
leads to a tendency to equate revelation with man's own best
insights. With no check on what constitutes revelation how can
it do other?

A Human Work

In much modern writing it is accepted that the Bible must
be seen as no more than the product of human insights and
human skill. James Barr puts it so well:

> My account of the formation of the biblical tradition is an
> account of a *human* work. It is *man's* statement of his beliefs,
> the events he has experienced, the stories he has been told,
> and so on. It has long been customary to align the Bible
> with concepts like Word of God, or revelation, and one
> effect of this has been to align the Bible with a movement
> *from God to man*. It is man who developed the biblical tradi-
> tion and man who decided when it might be suitably fixed
> and made canonical. If one wants to use the Word-of-God
> type of language, the proper term for the Bible would be
> Word of Israel, Word of some leading early Christians.[34]

He goes on to notice that this is not how the Bible itself views
things, but he thinks that we need not accept the Bible view.
   But it is precisely this that is in question. Why should we
not take with full seriousness the account the Bible writers
give of their Book? If they are wrong this should be demonstrated. It is not enough to say in effect, "This is not how I
would put it." It is an assumption that the Bible is a human
book, the product of the merely human imagination and that
it does not represent a movement from God to man. Of
course it can be countered that it is an assumption that it is
more than a human book. But any writing should be judged
in the first instance in the light of the claims it makes for itself.
A point I am very much concerned to make is that the Bible
claims to give us a message from God and that this claim

should be taken far more seriously than it is by many modern Christians.

Perhaps my point might be brought out with reference to another statement of Barr's, "The Pauline letters are letters from the apostle to the churches, not letters from God to St. Paul."[35] Put in this way the statement can scarcely be disputed. These letters are certainly not "from God to St. Paul". But who ever claimed that they were? Surely the claim that would be made is that they are letters from God to the churches through Paul. And who was this Paul? Certainly not a man who had grown up in isolation from God. He had been prepared by God for the work he was to do, including the writing of the letters that were to effect God's purpose. Let me quote some words I wrote a few years ago:

> If God wanted words like the Epistle to the Romans written, then I envisage Him as preparing a Paul to write them. He prepared him in his natural endowment. He prepared him in those years of which we know nothing. He prepared him in the years when Saul of Tarsus was a rising Jewish leader. He prepared him when he was persecuting the church. He prepared him by confronting him on the Damascus road, and transforming his whole conception of life and of God and of Jesus. He prepared him in the years that followed, in the quiet years of which we know nothing and in the active years of missionary service of which we know a little. He prepared him in the conflicts he had with the Judaizers and others. He prepared him in his daily discharge of "the care of all the churches". He prepared him in the depths of his soul in the spiritual lessons that all those years taught him. He prepared him by putting him in such a position vis-a-vis the Roman Church that it was the most natural thing for him, the Spirit-filled Apostle, to write as he did.[36]

I still think this important. We are not thinking of a little God, unable or unwilling to effect his purpose in the world he has made. We are thinking of a God who is the God of all of life, who is active ceaselessly in the affairs of men. His connection with Scripture should not be thought of as a kind of last minute brainwave, as though he suddenly conceived the idea of getting something written that might be useful. Rather, as in the words I have quoted, we are to think of God as preparing his agents through the years in all their dealings with him and with their fellow men. The result is words that are words of men. They express exactly what Paul or Peter or whoever wished to write. But there is more to it than that. They are the words of men but they are also the words of God, the words that God had prepared his servants to write. This Paul himself insists on several times and he is entitled to be heard. He tells the Corinthians, "we impart this in words not taught by human wisdom but taught by the Spirit" (1 Cor. 2: 13), and again, "If any one thinks that he is a prophet, or spiritual, he should acknowledge that what I am writing to you is a command of the Lord" (1 Cor. 14: 37). He looks back to the time of his preaching in Thessalonica and tells his converts that he thanks God "that when you received the word of God which you heard from us, you accepted it not as the word of men but as what it really is, the word of God" (1 Thess. 2: 13). We must not try to cut God down to size. He is able to effect his purpose through men and the contention of the Bible writers is that he has done just that. He has spoken through men.

In passing we may notice another suggestion of Barr's: "A Moses, an Isaiah, or a Paul was not given as his main task the work of producing tradition or of writing parts of the Bible." He goes on to say, "Their actual task was one of leadership in the community of their own time" and he sees the production of scripture as a "spin-off" from their leadership.[37] This may perhaps be the way of it, but it sounds a trifle too confident to me. And if Barr is right it must be borne in mind that God's purpose is realised in the "spin-off" just as it is in the leadership. I want to guard against the idea of a little God, unable to effect his purpose and who is taken by surprise when men he has raised up as leaders confront him with some scripture they have produced. The God we see in the Bible is a mighty God, a God well able to control the spin-off as well as the official functions of his people, and one who caused to be written such Scripture as he willed.

Another way of ruling out effectively any real revelation is that of making modern man the norm. Brevard Childs points out that we may do this, for example, by speaking of the activities of some contemporary as a "prophetic ministry". But the modern man does not hear the voice of God speaking to him directly as the prophets of old claim to have done. He does not and cannot say, "Hear the word of the Lord" in the same way as did the canonical prophets. If he were to say anything of the sort he would mean something like, "This is my considered conclusion, speaking as one with a profound sense of the importance of doing the will of God" (Childs, "This is what I as a sensitive religious person think").[38] Now if this is what he understands by it when used of his own day, he naturally reads the same meaning back into it when he uses the same phrase about the ministry of God's servant of old. Thus Isaiah or Amos or any of the others becomes no more than a good man giving his best insights into the situation in which he found himself. We have lost the genuine word of God and have settled for the best word of man.

In this chapter I have been concerned to insist that no method of studying the Bible is satisfactory that does not enable men to hear a genuine word from God. It is unfortunate that much of the excellent scholarly work being done in these days tends to hinder rather than help the humble men of faith. The scholars sometimes justify this. Thus Christopher Evans says, "As Käsemann observes, the piety of the pious cannot be allowed to have the last word." Presently he says it himself: "piety cannot have the last word with the Bible".[39] Without opting for obscurantism it is possible to differ. We must grant that there is a certain realm that properly belongs to the scholar and that in this he must not let himself be intimidated by the pious. But it is also true that Christianity is not an exercise in intellectualism, a kind of Gnosticism. The greatest scholars are not necessarily the greatest saints. History makes it abundantly clear that many of the most dedicated and profoundly spiritual saints have been far removed from the world of scholarship. A place must be found for them in Christianity and for the way they have nourished their profound piety by listening for God's voice in the Bible.

NOTES

1. J. V. Casserley, *Toward a Theology of History* (London: 1965), p. 116.
2. Paul S. Minear, *Interpretation*, Vol. xxvii (1973), p. 149.
3. William Temple, *Nature, Man and God* (London: 1964), p. 350.
4. J. V. Casserley, *Toward a Theology of History*, pp. 87f.
5. Brevard S. Childs, *Biblical Theology in Crisis* (Philadelphia: 1970), p. 141.

6. *Ibid.*, p. 142.
7. *Ibid.*, p. 147.
8. *The Bible Speaks Again* (London: 1969), p. 76.
9. *Ibid.*, p. 216.
10. J. V. Casserley, *Toward a Theology of History*, p. 91.
11. *Ibid.*, p. 123.
12. *Ibid.*
13. *Ibid.*, p. 105.
14. James S. Robinson, *A New Quest of the Historical Jesus* (London: 1959), p. 26.
15. *Ibid.*, p. 31.
16. G. E. Ladd, *Interpretation*, Vol. xxv (1971), pp. 51f.
17. Gerhard Kittel; G. K. A. Bell and A. Deissmann (eds.), *Mysterium Christi* (London: 1930), p. 49.
18. R. S. Barbour, *Traditio-Historical Criticism of the Gospels* (London: 1972), p. 35.
19. *Ibid.*, p. 37
20. *Ibid.*, p. 53, n. 47 (Barbour's italics).
21. Cited by Ladd, *Interpretation*, Vol. xxv, p. 58.
22. Ted Peters, *Catholic Biblical Quarterly*, Vol. xxxv (1973), pp. 475–82.
23. *Ibid.*, p. 475.
24. *Ibid.*, p. 481.
25. Quoted by Alfred Jepsen in *Essays on Old Testament Interpretation*, ed. Claus Westermann (London: 1963), p. 247.
26. *Ibid.*, p. 283.
27. *Ibid.*, p. 284.
28. James D. Smart, *The Strange Silence of the Bible in the Church* (London 1970), p. 27.
29. *Ibid.*, p. 41.
30. *Ibid.*, p. 42.
31. *Ibid.*, p. 70.
32. *Ibid.*, p. 141.
33. Cited by Bernard Ramm, *Special Revelation and the Word of God* (Grand Rapids: 1971), p. 52, n. 34.
34. James Barr, *The Bible in the Modern World* (London: 1973), p. 120 (Barr's italics).
35. *Ibid.*, p. 123.
36. Leon Morris, *The Truth of the Bible* (Sydney: 1958), p. 12.
37. James Barr, *The Bible in the Modern World*, p. 131.
38. Brevard Childs, *Bible Theology in Crisis* (Philadelphia: 1970), p. 101.
39. Christopher Evans, *Is "Holy Scripture" Christian?* (London: 1971), p. 38.

CHAPTER 6

Revelation and the Individual

MANY MODERN DISCUSSIONS reduce revelation, intentionally
or unintentionally, to a personal judgment of the individual.
It is the attitude of the reader of the Bible that is the decisive
factor. It is, of course, the case that there is always a subjective element when we read the Bible. No one can escape
his own subjectivity, least of all, may I say, the conservative.
But that does not mean that there is nothing beyond subjective experience.

One of the most frequently quoted and approved statements
on revelation is William Temple's famous dictum, *"What is
offered to man's apprehension in any specific Revelation is not truth
concerning God but the living God Himself."*[1] This sounds very
attractive to the modern student. It liberates him from bondage
to the letter of the Bible. And it allows him to make direct
contact with God in the moment of revelation, or at the
least to feel that the men of the Bible had this direct contact,
however fallibly they may have reported what they experienced.

But if when we come to the Bible we find no "truth concerning God" what do we find? Fine words about "the living
God Himself" cannot conceal the fact that we are left with
our own experience of God (or that of the Bible writers).
It is the human response that we have in the Bible and not
the revelation itself. When we read the Bible rightly we may
have an encounter with God. But on this view it is the
encounter, not the Bible that is important. There is nothing
of the "whether they hear or whether they forbear" of the
prophets. It is our own personal attitude that is important,
indeed decisive.

So with the Barthian approach. For Karl Barth himself,

the Bible is "God's Word so far as God lets it be His Word".[2]
Emil Brunner speaks of man as experiencing "the working
of the Holy Spirit as a real utterance of God" and proceeds,
"Only in this Word of the Holy Spirit does the Divine revelation in Jesus Christ become the real, actual word of God to
man."[3] How do we know this "real, actual word of God to
man"? Only it would seem by our subjective experience of
the Holy Spirit. Is there any way we can discern the revelation
other than by introspection?

Deeds Rather than Words

A way of viewing revelation which at first sight gives promise
of objectivity is that which affirms that the revelation is not
to be found in words but in deeds. The revelation is shifted
from the words of the Bible to the deeds those words record.
Leonard Hodgson holds that revelation "is given primarily
not in words but in deeds, in events which become revelatory
to us as the Holy Spirit opens our eyes to see their significance
as acts of God".[4] But examination reveals this approach to
be just as subjective as those we have just looked at. For
when we ask, "How are we to discern the revelation in the
deeds?" the only answer appears to be "By the way we think
about them". In the case of Hodgson himself this is not in
doubt. He says, "such objectivity as we have a right to expect
will come as a result of scholars putting alongside of one
another their various readings of the evidence, each saying
to the rest: "This is how I see it. Cannot you see it too?"[5]
If Hodgson is right this is all we have. But it is not objectivity.
It is putting ourselves into the hands of the experts who have
nothing more than their own subjective apprehension of the
truth.

A further objection to this view, and one which is not usually
faced by those who put it forward, is that a series of unexplained
acts is not revelation. "An event reveals nothing and nobody
apart from some understanding of its significance."[6] Some
Hebrews escaped from Egypt rather against the will of the
reigning Pharaoh. A certain Amos looked out on society
and vigorously denounced the evils he saw. A peasant from
Nazareth was executed by crucifixion during the governor-
ship of Pontius Pilate. But none of these facts, of itself, is
revelation. Paul Minear asks, "How could a bystander in
Jerusalem, watching one of the innumerable executions beyond
the city wall, detect that scene as one decisive for all human

history?"[7] If we took the united testimony of all who took part in the crucifixion we could not arrive at an understanding of what was there revealed. For that we need the inspired interpretation. So with the other events in the Bible. The great majority of the people of the day who knew of them did not see them as revelation. For that matter, large numbers of people do not see them as revelation to this day. For revelation to be discerned the right interpretation is needed. It is necessary that someone who knows come and say, "This is what God has done in these events. This is what God is saying to men through those happenings." Apart from such an interpretation they remain a series of more or less interesting happenings and no more. Until modern times Christians have always understood that the Bible writers were inspired to give us this interpretation. The revelation has been seen in the inspired interpretation rather than in the acts themselves, or perhaps in the acts plus the revelation. But certainly the interpretation has always been seen as a necessity if we are to receive the revelation. The deeds by themselves are not enough.

Bernard Ramm makes the interesting point that, while most of us would choose deafness rather than blindness, blind people do not suffer as much from emotional disturbances as do the deaf.

> The warm personal relationships of life are carried on by means of conversation, and the deaf man is largely severed from those relationships. The soundless world is far more frustrating than the sightless world. Radio drama is entertaining but a television drama robbed of the sound track is drained of all meaning. *In life as in drama it is the word which carries the meaning; it is the word which is the element of cohesion; and it is the word which is the necessary presupposition for warm personal friendships.*[8]

Actions without words usually tell us little. For precision of meaning words are necessary. A view of revelation that concentrates on deeds to the exclusion of words will always be found wanting. P. Benoit sees hearing as more significant than vision: "The visual register is not the only one in the biblical register of revelation. There is also the aural, which is much more important. Here it is the word of God that reverberates."[9]

Inspired Authors

Just as some shift the revelation from the words to the deeds, so some shift it from the words to the authors who wrote the words. Inspiration is predicated not of the Bible but of the men who wrote the Bible. They caught a vision of God and proceeded to write it down with the best of the faulty words they could muster. They are often held to have been wrong and their vision partial at best. In passing we should notice that this is not the way it is put in 2 Timothy 3:16. There it is "all scripture" that is said to be inspired, not the writers. Indeed the writers are not even mentioned.

One objection to this view may be put in the words of John Baillie:

> Nothing could be more artificial than to suppose that these writers were endowed with infallibility in all that they had in mind to say, while the Holy Spirit left them to their own devices as to how they should say it. Hence on the other hand we should have no hesitation in affirming that inspiration extended not only to the thought of the writers, but to the very words they employed in the expression of these thoughts.[10]

To say the least, it would be a curious procedure if God inspired these men with tremendous ideas of permanent significance and then left it to the men themselves to express these tremendous ideas in their own inadequate way. Benoit speaks of the "strange sacrifices" some scholars find it necessary to make, "such as the renunciation of the inspiration of the words in order to safeguard the revelation of the ideas".[11] This is indeed a strange sacrifice. We need strong evidence before accepting such a view.

This way of looking at the Bible is but one more route to subjectivism. Isaiah say, or Paul may have had a clear vision of God or of some truth about God. But on this view neither Isaiah's prophecy nor Paul's epistles gives us this revelation. For that we must ask ourselves some such question as "What must the truth about God be if men like Isaiah or Paul wrote like this?" And our answer will begin, "This is the way it seems to me."

Encounter

Sometimes it is suggested that revelation is essentially encounter. The propositions laid down in Scripture are un-important, even irrelevant. What matters is the encounter the man of faith has with God. There is truth here. It cannot be denied that men may meet God, nor that this meeting is a revelation to them. John Baillie puts it this way:

> I could not know that God had revealed Himself to the prophets and apostles through these events, unless through His revelation of Himself to them He were now revealing Himself to me. I could know indeed that they claimed to have received such a revelation, but I can know that their claim was justified only if, as I read what they say, I too find myself in the presence of God.[12]

Our commitment as we respond to the revelation is im-portant. And it may well be that as a result of that commitment we become sure that it is revelation we are encountering. But it is neither the commitment nor the encounter that is the revelation. Unless God has taken an initiative and revealed the way men may meet him, how are they going to meet him? Men cannot decide "We will now meet God" and the thing is done. God discloses himself when and as he wills. He may, of course, choose to reveal himself directly at any time. I know a man who says that he had no faith, no religion of any sort, until God spoke to him one day as he sat in the park. Such encounters cannot be ruled out. But it appears that God has chosen normally to link his self-disclosure to a book. He has given the Bible as the means whereby men have access to him and we ignore this at our peril. To say that revelation is encounter and leave it at that is to mis-understand what revelation means.

Propositional Revelation
That the revelation is propositional is a contention held with the utmost tenacity and opposed with the utmost fierceness. In some quarters "opposed" would be the wrong word. It is considered so impossible and out of date as not to be worth opposing.

If by "propositional revelation" is meant that certain propositions have been divinely revealed and laid up in a book and that this is the whole story, then the concept is rightly rejected. It is important to be clear that redemption is prior to revelation. The whole Old Testament is to be seen in terms of God's gracious provision for his people's needs, his mighty acts in history and the preparation for the coming of his Son. The New Testament continues the story and records the saving acts in the life, death, resurrection and ascension of Jesus. It goes on to the preaching and interpretation of these acts in the early church. It is the meeting of the needs of sinful men that is steadily in mind throughout, not the production of a sacred book which is to be revered. Indeed E. Carnell can go as far as to say, "To conceive of the Bible as the primary revelation is heresy. If there had been no redemptive events, there would be no theology."[13]

We have rejected the idea that the essence of revelation is encounter, but encounter is important nevertheless. The significant thing is that men be brought face to face with God, that they realise their need, repent of their sin, believe and commit themselves to the life of service of their God and of their fellowmen. The Bible is but the means to that end. It is not to be revered for itself or venerated as a religious object produced by a divine process so that men may accord it due respect. It is no more than a means. It is the means whereby men may learn of God and of themselves and of the way they can come into right relationship with God. It is the means whereby they may realise their lost state and find salvation in Christ. This cannot be emphasised too strongly.

But to go on from there that revelation is not propositional is another thing altogether. Christianity is not a philosophy, a starting point for a debate about men's ideas. It is basically a gospel, "good news". And "good news" has content. It could not be good news otherwise. Bernard Ramm lays it down that "*what the inept phrase 'propositional revelation' intends, or means, is also accepted in principle by its critics*".[14] He goes on to explain, "The phrase intends that there is a valid conceptual side to revelation." It is hard to see how this is to be resisted, unless we are prepared to reduce revelation to some misty, undefined concept which leaves us perpetually in doubt as to whether we do in fact know God or not.

To hold to propositional revelation is not to insist that the Bible is a series of infallible propositions laid side by side for our inspection and assimilation. Some of the Bible may well be held to come under this description, as for example the proposition, "God is love" (1 John 4: 8). But much of the Bible is not susceptible of this kind of treatment. Often the exegete must wrestle with difficult problems if he is to come up with the meaning of the text. Most of us would agree that no superficial study can do justice to say, the Book of Job or the Epistle to the Romans. While there is a surface meaning such that anybody can read such books to their immediate profit, there is also a profundity such that much patient labour must go into their study. The deepest meaning becomes apparent only after years of close study. To speak of propositional revelation is not to deny this. Nor is it to deny that due regard must be had to the differences in interpretation needed for the study of poetry, parable, history and the rest.

But it is to insist that, when due regard is had to all the proper procedures of the exegete, what he comes up with has conceptual content. It is capable of being given expression.

Indeed this is essential to any real revelation of a person. When much modern theology denies propositional revelation but insists that revelation is a revelation of God himself it is not easy to see what is meant. As Hugo Meynell puts it, "The contention that revelation is primarily of a person, and not of propositions, is not to the point; since *that* God is revealed as a person, and *what* kind of person it is that God is revealed to be, and *how* he is so revealed, can be expressed only in propositions."[15] How can we know God unless we know something about him? What is meant by such knowledge? On the human level I know a number of persons and in each case I know something about the person in question. I cannot say that I know the person unless I can also say that I have knowledge of some facts about that person. I find it hard to imagine what it would be to claim knowledge of a person about whom I know nothing. Even on casual acquaintance I know something, for example the appearance of the person and what he reveals by his words and actions.

So with God. If I know nothing about him it is difficult to put content into the sentence, "I know God." The more I can know about him the more I can know him. This is not to reduce the knowledge of God to a set of propositions. Knowing a person means more than knowing about him. But knowing about him is an indispensable part of knowing him. This is, of course, elementary and obvious. It would scarcely be worth saying were it not for the fact that in their depreciation of propositional revelation some critics seem to lose sight of it.

Fortunately it is being widely realised that the battle against propositional revelation is pointless. Thus James Barr, no friend of conservative opinions, points out that those who oppose propositional revelation usually shift their ground at points of difficulty. "For instance, they often begin by opposing a 'propositional' view and then go on to say that the Bible is not concerned with 'timeless truths'."[16] Barr is surely right when he says, "But this is obviously a different matter." There is a similar shift when people object to propositional revelation and go on to object to the view that the Bible consists of abstract propositions. Obviously propositions need be neither timeless nor abstract. In both cases the argument has moved from propositions to a particular kind of proposition. As Barr says, the issue "seems mostly to have been not an issue about propositions (as against non-propositional communication) but one about the recognition of the *right function* of propositions (along with non-propositional verbal communications)."[17] While Barr is not arguing for the traditional view of propositional revelation his recognition of the nonsense that has sometimes been used in opposition to it is timely.

Barr has some words about "verbal inspiration" which are relevant. He does not, of course, accept it, but he thinks it not unreasonable that the earlier theologians did. He goes on,

> The quest for a formulation which will do justice to the status of the Bible but avoid the connotations of the word "verbal", such as *plenary inspiration*, inspiration of the *ideas*, inspiration of the *authors*, inspiration of the *inner theology*, and so on, is just no longer important. What we know about the authors, the ideas, the inner theology and so on is known ultimately from the verbal form of the Bible. As in any other literary work, the verbal form is its mode of communicating meaning. If the verbal form of the Bible were different, then its meaning would be different.[18]

This must be insisted upon. The precise form of words is important. We must be careful how we express our views on inspiration, inerrancy and the like. But unless we conclude that the words used have their significance we are bound to end up with an unsatisfactory formulation. To affirm the necessary place of the knowledge conveyed by propositions is not to give way to an arid intellectualism. It is to realise that there is a right place for the mind as well as the heart in our approach to God.

It is God's gracious act in saving men that is primary. The Bible is of use only in that it brings us into contact with that saving act and with the God who saves. But it is of use for these purposes and it is not easy to see how we would be brought into saving knowledge of God without it.

It seems necessary that the revelation be preserved in a written form. For a while, it is true, parts of it at any rate were handed on orally. But there are too many possibilities of distortion for this to be the permanent solution. We need not be surprised that the revelation is in writing.

For some in our day this is a hard saying. They see life and written scripture as in necessary conflict. If we are to have the freedom of the Spirit we cannot be dominated by the letter of a written record. But this is our tension, not that of the men of the Bible. Jesus could say, "the words that I have spoken to you are spirit and life" (John 6: 63). Paul, it is true, contrasts the new covenant "in the Spirit" with a written code (2 Cor. 3: 6). But to take the Bible seriously is not to reduce it to "a written code", a series of prescriptions that must be taken with strict literalness. That is a Koran, not a Bible. It is God's saving activity that is the primary thing and the record of what God has done and what he asks of men is not to be reduced to "a written code". There is no contradiction between Jesus and Paul. Both are repudiating a Koran-type approach. Both are saying that there is real life in the "words" of Jesus, that we have "the light of the knowledge of the glory of God in the face of Christ" (2 Cor. 4: 6).

Th. C. Vriezen argues strongly for the place of the word in revelation even as he insists on the centrality of personal relationships.

> The word as an element of revelation bears witness to the direct personal relationship between God and man as well as to the spiritual nature of this relationship. By the word the deepest feelings of one man can find an echo in the heart of another, even without any physical manifestation or contact; although, of course, a gesture or personal presence may strengthen the impression created by the word. This is proof of the spiritual importance of the word, which as a phenomenon is as great a secret as life itself and which may be considered the essential feature of man's spiritual life.[19]

It is not easy to see how this can be resisted. Rational intercourse depends on the use of words. And it is the right use of words that leads us into the inner being of another. Without the right words we are always stumbling. We need not, accordingly, be surprised at the place words occupy in the revelation. They are God's way of making his truth known to his people.

This direct word of God does not mean that the prophets (or any other recipients of revelation) found revelation easy. As we read through the troubled narratives of Hosea and Jeremiah and Amos and the rest it is clear that even these giants of the faith had their problems in finding the right way. They saw some things with crystal clarity and did not budge on such matters as the greatness of God's love or the certainty of God's judgment. But relating such great truths to the circumstances in which they found themselves was not easy and they were often perplexed and sometimes downcast. But the problems and perplexities of the prophets did not prevent God's word being recorded. And it need not prevent later generations from apprehending it. The realisation that the prophets and others were caught up on the same "cussedness of things" as we are and that yet God spoke to and through them makes our own struggle more meaningful.

The importance of the words must be stressed. It is only in the measure that we can trust the record that we can apprehend the revelation. If we cannot believe the record we cannot recover the acts of God or the inspired thinking of the writers. We can find only our own ideas about what those acts and that thinking must be. We are dependent on the Bible for the revelation. Apart from the Bible we do not know it. If the Bible does not give it to us in trustworthy form then we do not have it in trustworthy form. Karl Barth might distinguish between what God said and what Paul said, between a *Deus dixit* and a *Paulus dixit*. But we know the *Deus dixit* through the *Paulus dixit*. And (with the necessary addition of the other biblical writers) we know it no other way.

A Priori *Ideas of Revelation*

I have been objecting to a variety of views of revelation on the ground that they are too subjective. It is well, accordingly, to notice that many recent writers bring the charge of subjectivity against conservative views. The conservatives, they suggest, demand from God the kind of revelation they think they ought to have instead of being content with the one God has seen fit to grant us. For example, C. F. Evans warns us against

> any sentence which begins with the words "Surely God would have . . ." for it is a religious *a priori* sentence. "Surely God would have seen to it that the Bible would have been preserved from error." "Surely God would have seen to it that there would be an instrument on earth which would teach without error." This is how the sentences run which are spoken from the embattled positions. But for all their impressiveness must they not be judged irreligious and heretical sentences?[20]

To this we must reply with a hearty "Amen". Perhaps "heretical" is too strong a word, but the position must certainly be repudiated. Indeed, entering into the spirit of the thing we might add one or two more to Evans's forbidden sentences. "Surely God would have put no distinction between writing then and now." "Surely God would not have made an objective, once-for-all revelation to which all should give heed." "Surely God would not have caused definitive, inerrant Scriptures to be written in Bible days but only casual and errant writings in our day." Are not these sentences also spoken from embattled positions? Are they not just as irreligious and heretical as those Evans abhors?

The fact is that we are in no position to say whether revelation will occur or not, and, if it does, how it will occur. We cannot lay it down dogmatically that God will reveal himself, nor that if he does it will be in an infallible book, nor that it will be in a fallible book. We can only accept with a proper humility what God has in fact chosen to give us. We must not start with the assumption that the Bible must necessarily be no more than a piece of ancient literature just like other ancient literature or from the opposite assumption that it must necessarily be different.

The question is "What has God done?" Here the conservative refuses to manufacture a theory of revelation. He does not start with a fixed view of what must be and proceed to work from that. He does not assume that the Bible writings must be of the same kind as other writings of that day (or of our day). Or for that matter that they must be different.

He is content to take the facts as they are. The point must be emphasised as the contrary is so often asserted. It is suggested that the conservative is a man with a sense of something lacking, who clamours for an infallible authority. He must find infallibility somewhere, so he casts about until he happens upon Scripture.

I imagine that the conservative is no more free from deep-seated yearnings than other men, but this is not in fact how he reaches his ideas on revelation. He turns to Christ and Christ's apostles and asks what they have to say on the matter. He tries to take his view of revelation from them. He holds that the Christian view of revelation, as of other doctrines, is the view of Christ, the view that Christ held and passed on to his apostles, the view which the apostles in their turn taught the church. The conservative sees the Bible as the authentic revelation, for that is the teaching he derives from Christ. If he is to be persuaded to abandon it this will not be by dogmatic assertions about his deep-seated needs and lacks and desires, but by showing either that this is not the teaching of Jesus or that there is some reason why the teaching of Jesus should not be followed in this case. But we should be clear that he gets his view from Jesus. It is not his own view. It is not the result of some subjective process.

He fears that the same cannot usually be said about the view of his more radical brother. The latter makes no claim to submitting to Christ or to anyone else in this matter. Rather he works out his concept of revelation according to his best insights. He may take notice of what Christ said or what the apostles said or what his colleagues say. But in the last resort his view of revelation is simply that which commends itself to him. His reasoning seems completely subjective.

An Incredible View
Such a view of revelation as Jesus and his apostles taught is thought by many these days to be quite impossible. Such views were all very well in antiquity, runs the reasoning, but the concept of a reliable Bible containing God's message for all time is one which we can no longer hold. It is frankly incredible.

This is a somewhat curious argument in an age like our own. The scientific world picture might equally well be called "frankly incredible". According to our scientists the world is not, for example, a place of brilliant colours as we imagine.

There are light waves of differing lengths that fall on our eyes. This starts a process the end result of which is that our brains interpret the sensations we receive as colour. On the evidence the scientist is right. But his world picture is not one that would have occurred to the non-scientist or even one which the non-scientist can revel in when it is explained to him. So with the scientific view of matter. The physicist assures us that there is no such thing as solid matter. He speaks of protons, electrons and the like and in the end apparently reduces even these to a set of mathematical equations.

But that is not the way it all seems to us. We find the scientific world view so incredible that, unless we are dedicated scientists, we hold it only when the facts are being drawn to our attention. At other times we simply go on as though the scientific view was completely false and keep on thinking of the world as a place where there are such things as colour and solid matter. In the end we accept the scientific view. The facts allow us no alternative. But it is the facts alone that compel us. It is certainly not the way we would have thought things are.

It is something like this with revelation. The conservative holds his view, not on *a priori* grounds, not because he finds this view naturally attractive, but because the facts constrain him. Of course in this area we are not moving among facts which are capable of demonstration in the same manner as a scientific experiment. For this reason we can never expect the same unanimity as with the scientific world view. Some will dispute the facts as the conservative sees them. All I am saying is that the conservative follows the evidence as well as he can and holds his view on the basis of that evidence. When his radical brother says that his view is incredible he retorts that it is no more incredible than the scientific picture of the world. Indeed it is considerably less so. But his respect for the facts allows him to take up no other position. He has no *a priori* conviction that revelation must take place in this way or that. Nor has he an *a priori* view of the kind of resemblance that will appear between the Bible and other writings. It is the facts of the teaching of Jesus and his apostles that carry conviction.

The Holy Spirit

There are difficulties in the way of accepting the view that it is only when the Holy Spirit takes the words of the Bible that they become the word of God. But that does not mean that we should minimise the place of the Spirit. We do not recognise the truth of the Bible without his work within us. While Scripture is objectively the word of God and remains so whether we accept it or reject it, it is the inner witness of the Spirit that brings conviction. This is all the more so in that the essential revelation of the Gospel is so uncongenial to man. In other areas of life such as science or philosophy to be confronted with a new "revelation" is to accept it with delight. There is an attractiveness about new knowledge. But the basic revelation in the gospel is that man is a sinner, who of himself can do nothing to merit his salvation. Salvation comes as God's gift in the saving work of the incarnate Son of God. It takes nothing less than the power of the Holy Spirit to bring that home to man.

It is only as the believer responds to this leading of the Holy Spirit that he understands the revelation for what it is. Apart from the freedom the Spirit gives he may well see the revelation as an assortment of truths committed to him which he must fiercely defend to the end. Life becomes a battle, but it is not so much the good fight of faith as a battle to keep our piece of religious real estate safe in the face of the opposition of those who would dispossess us. We then display not a militant faith but a piece of touchiness in standing up for our spiritual possessions as we see them.

This is not Christianity. Christians are rather men who have been seized by the revelation, caught up by the power of God. The revelation is not some impersonal thing in which they have come to have a detached intellectual interest. It is something to which believers are committed. We cannot bank our capital of belief. We must live on it. We are existentially committed to the revelation.

There is a sense in which our experience of the revelation is a living and a growing thing. In the words of P. T. Forsyth, "We receive our legacy under conditions of active tenancy and yearly improvements. The sure Christ of our frolic youth would not be a sufficient certainty for our tragic old age."[21] As we go on from strength to strength the revelation proceeds from glory to glory. We prove it on an increasingly deep level all the way. I do not wish to deny this aspect of revelation when I insist on its objective character. Its objectivity is consistent with important subjective aspects. Indeed, we know more and more of the revelation as we make subjective experience of it. But our subjective experience does not create it. It does no more than enable us to apprehend it.

We must respond then to the way the Spirit leads us as he makes the revelation live for us. But we must bear in mind that at times people have done the most curious things, maintaining all the while that what they have done they have done in response to the leading of the Spirit. When men claim the leading of the Spirit I do not see how it can be decided whether they are right or not otherwise than by reference to Scripture. It is this that enables us to test the spirits. Back of it all is the Bible. What does not agree with Scripture has no claim to the title "revelation".

Objective Exegesis

An objection that is always raised sooner or later is that "You can prove anything from the Bible". There is inevitably an element of presupposition in all our understanding of Scripture and it is held that this vitiates exegesis. While an objective standard is in theory highly desirable, in practice it proves decidedly difficult of attainment.

It cannot be denied that some curious "exegesis" takes place. We are all far too ready to see our own ideas in Scripture and we tend to understand difficult or doubtful passages in ways that agree with our basic position rather than in ways that oppose us. Yet this cannot be the last word. If it were, scholarly discussion would be completely impossible. Yet every day of the year scholars carry on their researches and produce their monographs confident that others will see something valid in what they are doing. They all have their presuppositions. But they have learned to live with them and to make allowances for them. In the practice of their discipline they carry out a scientific examination of the passages before them, relying on grammar, context and the like. If this could not be done then biblical scholarship would be impossible and we would be through with all rational discussion of religious questions. Fortunately it is not necessary to draw this devastating conclusion. Granted that none of us is perfect in his exegesis, yet we know enough about how to proceed for a meaningful understanding of Scripture to emerge.

Of course we are never perfect in this, just as we are never perfect in our struggle against temptation. But the fact that we do not attain sinlessness does not discourage us from trying to live out the implications of our faith. And our exegetical shortcomings should not convince us that the whole enterprise is valueless. Some passages are, of course, such that with our present information we must not expect agreement. But this is not the case with Scripture as a whole. The possibility of honest, unprejudiced exegesis is that which makes the whole of biblical studies possible.

Smart cites Bernard E. Meland, "There is really no such thing as *purely* objective inquiry, that is, inquiry in which the interested, centred existence of the inquirer plays no part. At best there is a disciplined use of our powers in which the bias of interest and conditioning are brought reasonably under control."[22] But this latter is attainable and its importance must not be under-emphasised. There is no reason why what the man is should not help him interpret the text. But there is also no reason why he should not make reasonable allowances for his bias and produce an exegesis which will commend itself not only to himself but also to his colleagues. Scripture is not a nose of wax which may be twisted in any direction at the whim of the exegete. There is an objectivity about the meaning of any Bible passage which the exegete is bound to respect.

Variety

Is it necessary to point out that this does not mean compressing the rich variety of the Bible into some monochrome theological straightjacket? This chapter is basically concerned with the objectivity and the subjectivity which are both part of our reading of Scripture. But it may be in place to notice that often those who take the Bible seriously are accused of forcing passages with divergent meanings into an unnatural harmony, with manufacturing a unity where none exists in the original. Such practices must be vigorously eschewed. It is important that each passage be allowed to speak for itself whether it says what the exegete expects it to say or not, and whether it agrees with what the exegete thinks some other passage is saying or not.

Let me give an example. In each of the first two Gospels there is but one saying of Jesus from the cross, "My God, my God, why hast thou forsaken me?" (Matt. 27:46; Mark 15:34). In Luke, however, the dying Saviour says trustfully, "Father, into thy hands I commend my spirit" (Luke 23:46). It is possible to spend a lot of ingenuity trying to make these two sayings agree with one another. But in my opinion this is to handle the Bible without integrity. Rather we should let each Evangelist speak for himself whether we can harmonise what he says with the others or not and whether we think we should try to harmonise the sayings or not. Matthew and Mark are telling us that Jesus died a terrible death, a death in which he was forsaken by the Father. Luke is saying something quite different. He is saying that in his death Jesus did the will of the Father (Luke 22: 42); it was quite natural accordingly for him to commit himself to the Father as he died. It may be that we can bring these together, perhaps by saying that it was the Father's will that Jesus should die the terrible death of forsakenness as the way in which sinners were to be saved: Mark brings out the foresakenness and Luke the unity of will between Father and Son. It may be that this is not the way we should approach it. My point is that, whether we are interested in harmonisations or not, we must not gloss over the meaning of what Scripture says, nor seek to minimise the interesting variety we find there.

There is a unity about the Bible as it reveals to us one God and no more. But there is also a variety of ways in which men view that one God and we must blind ourselves to none of them. The unity is important and the diversity is important. But individual preferences should blind us to neither.

NOTES

1. William Temple, *Nature, Man and God* (London: 1964), p. 322 (Temple's italics).
2. Karl Barth, *Church Dogmatics*, Vol. 1. (Edinburgh: 1955) Part 1, p. 213.
3. Emil Brunner, *The Christian Doctrine of God* (London: 1949), p. 30.
4. Leonard Hodgson, *On the Authority of the Bible*, S.P.C.K. Theological Collections, no. 1 (London: 1960), p. 4.
5. *Ibid.*, p. 10.
6. A. Snell, *Truth in Words* (London: 1965), p. 63.
7. Cited by B. Ramm, *Special Revelation and the Word of God* (Grand Rapids: 1971), p. 77.
8. *Ibid.*, p. 78 (Ramm's italics).
9. P. Benoit, *Inspiration and the Bible* (London: 1965), p. 30.
10. John Baillie, *The Idea of Revelation in Recent Thought* (Oxford: 1956), p. 115.
11. P. Benoit, *Inspiration and the Bible*, p. 94.
12. John Baillie, *The Idea of Revelation in Recent Thought*, p. 105.

13. E. Carnell, *The Case for Orthodox Theology* (Philadelphia: 1959), p. 49.
14. B. Ramm, *Special Revelation and the Word of God*, p. 154.
15. Hugo Meynell, *The Journal of Theological Studies*, new series, Vol. xxiv, (1973), p. 157 (Meynell's italics).
16. James Barr, *The Bible in the Modern World* (London: 1973), p. 123.
17. *Ibid.*, p. 125.
18. *Ibid.*, p. 178.
19. Th. C. Vriezen, *An Outline of Old Testament Theology* (Oxford: 1962), p. 253.
20. C. F. Evans, *On the Authority of the Bible*, S.P.C.K. *Theological Collections*, no. 4 (London: 1960), p. 73.
21. P. T. Forsyth, *The Principle of Authority* (London: 1952), p. 32.
22. Bernard E. Meland cited by Smart, *The Strange Silence of the Bible in the Church* (London: 1970), pp. 178f., n. 19.

CHAPTER 7

Salvation and Scripture

CHRISTIANITY IS A religion about a cross. It is absolutely central that Jesus died to bring men salvation. Without that what we have is not the Christian faith. Paul Althaus brings out the point by saying, "Golgotha is not everywhere, but in Jerusalem, and the day of Jesus' death was a particular day. On that day something happened that does not continue, and does not happen when the kerygma is preached, but happened once, and once for all."[1] It is basic that it is God who saves, not man. There is a significant remark in the Preface to the symposium, *Revelation and the Bible*. After claiming that the contributors avoid many of the reactionary defences of the past the Preface goes on, "Rather, they discuss Biblical revelation with full reference to God's saving acts and thereby contemplate revealed ideas in association with redemptive history."[2] The "saving acts" are just that. They are "saving". We must not think of God's mighty acts as so much pageantry, a show wherein God simply reveals himself. They are God in action saving men.

This has been clear from the first. The message to Timothy was "from childhood you have been acquainted with the sacred writings which are able to instruct you for salvation through faith in Christ Jesus" (2 Tim. 3: 15). The whole purpose of the sacred writings was to bring men to the salvation that is in Christ. Jesus himself said to the Jews on one occasion, "You search the scriptures, because you think that in them you have eternal life; and it is they that bear witness to me; yet you refuse to come to me that you may have life" (John 5: 39f.). The Jews often had a wooden reverence for the literal meaning of the Bible. Their attitude was not acceptable, but Jesus is saying to them that had they really relied on the Bible and accepted its testimony to himself they would have found life. It is not material things that bring life but "everything that proceeds out of the mouth of the Lord" (Deut. 8: 3), words which Jesus quoted at the time of his temptation (Matt. 4: 4); in passing we notice that in the temptation Jesus was sustained by the words of his Bible, not, as we might have supposed, by his communion with the Father or the like).

The Words of Jesus

It is not only the words of the Father but the words of Jesus Christ also that have importance in connection with salvation. We read that he said, "whoever is ashamed of me and of my words in this adulterous and sinful generation, of him will the Son of man also be ashamed, when he comes in the glory of his Father with the holy angels" (Mark 8: 38). If our eternal destiny hinges on our attitude to Jesus' words then it is obviously of the first importance that we have access to those words. The same truth is put in another way: "My mother and my brothers are those who hear the word of God and do it" (Luke 8: 21). This refers, of course, to the word of God rather than to that of Jesus. But the passage is saying that right relationship to Jesus is determined, not by family connection and the like but by attention to "the word of God".

It is interesting to see a similar stress on the words of Jesus in the Fourth Gospel, for this Gospel has often been regarded not as serious history but as the considered teaching of the author on a number of topics important to an understanding of the Christian faith. But this Gospel has many statements like this one: "If I tell the truth, why do you not believe me? He who is of God hears the words of God; the reason why you do not hear them is that you are not of God" (John 8: 46f.). Here we are told that the words of Jesus are the words of God. If this is the considered opinion of the writer after years of meditation on the Christian message it seems to follow that those words are sufficiently important to be given us and not replaced by the evangelist's own version of what the teaching ought to be. The more it is insisted that this Gospel reflects the result of prolonged meditation on the essence of the Christian faith, the more difficult it is to escape the conclusion that those words are important

enough to be recorded. Of course, we must bear in mind
that Jesus probably spoke in Aramaic and that the Gospels
are written in Greek so that we must always allow for an
element of interpretation as the words are translated. But
we should not exaggerate this. It is possible to translate
without re-writing the original. The point is important
because of the frequent stress on Jesus' words in this Gospel.
Consider the following:

Truly, truly, I say to you, he who hears my word and
believes him who sent me, has eternal life (5: 24).

the words that I have spoken to you are spirit and life
(6: 63).

My teaching is not mine, but his who sent me; if any man's
will is to do his will, he shall know whether the teaching
is from God or whether I am speaking on my own authority
(7: 16f.).

I speak of what I have seen with my Father (8: 38).

Why do you not understand what I say? It is because
you cannot bear to hear my word . . . He who is of God
hears the words of God; the reason why you do not hear
them is that you are not of God (8: 43-7).

My sheep hear my voice, and I know them, and they follow
me; and I give them eternal life (10: 27f.).

He who rejects me and does not receive my sayings has a
judge; the word that I have spoken will be his judge on the
last day (12: 48).

What I say, therefore, I say as the Father has bidden me
(12: 50).

The words that I say to you I do not speak on my own
authority; but the Father who dwells in me does his
works (14: 10).

If you love me, you will keep my commandments . . . He

who has my commandments and keeps them, he it is who
loves me. . . . If a man loves me, he will keep my word.
. . . He who does not love me does not keep my words;
and the word which you hear is not mine but the Father's
who sent me (14: 15, 21, 23, 24).

the Counsellor, the Holy Spirit, whom the Father will
send in my name, he will teach you all things, and bring
to your remembrance all that I have said to you (14: 26).

If you abide in me, and my words abide in you, ask whatever you will, and it shall be done for you (15: 7).

If you keep my commandments, you will abide in my
love (15: 10).

No longer do I call you servants, for the servant does not
know what his master is doing; but I have called you
friends, for all that I have heard from my Father I have
made known to you (15: 15).

I have given them the words which thou gavest me, and
they have received them and know in truth that I came
from thee (17: 8).

thy word is truth (17: 17).

It is difficult to think that this constant stress on the "words"
of Christ or of God is consistent with the view that the teaching of Jesus is recorded with scant regard to what the Master
actually said. One can imagine a mystic who brooded over
the teaching of Jesus and in the end came up with an account
in which his own thinking was inextricably mixed up with
the teaching of Jesus. But it is more than difficult to think
that the end result of such a process would be the kind of
emphasis on the words of Jesus which the Fourth Gospel in
fact yields.
    Sometimes we get the other side of the coin, as when we
learn that the teacher who "does not agree with the sound
words of our Lord Jesus Christ and the teaching which accords
with godliness" is "puffed up with conceit, he knows nothing;
he has a morbid craving for controversy and for disputes
about words, which produce envy, dissension, slander, base

suspicions, and wrangling among men who are depraved in
mind and bereft of the truth, imagining that godliness is a
means of gain" (1 Tim. 6: 3-5). This is a trifle hard on the
teachers in question if in fact there is no way of knowing
what "the sound words of our Lord Jesus Christ" are. The
presupposition is that the teaching is available, and the later
we date 1 Timothy the more likely it is that this teaching was
embodied in written documents.

The Word of the Church
It is the claim of Paul that Christian teachers speak "in words
not taught by human wisdom but taught by the Spirit"
(1 Cor. 2: 13). He thanks God that the Thessalonians received
"the word of God which you heard from us" not "as the
word of men but as what it really is, the word of God" (1 Thess.
2: 13). It is only this assurance that enables him to write,
"If any one refuses to obey what we say in this letter, note
that man, and have nothing to do with him" (2 Thess. 3: 14).
If what he is writing is no more than the words of a man this
is an incredibly egotistic statement. Its justification surely
lies in the earlier passages cited—Paul is sure that what he
is writing to the Thessalonian church is God's word for them,
not merely his own insights.

And it is this word which Jesus committed to the church
and which justifies it in its proclamation of its message as
divine. In the Upper Room he prayed for his immediate
followers but also for others: "I do not pray for these only,
but also for those who believe in me through their word"
(John 17: 20). Once again it is the "word" which Jesus
gave them (John 17: 8) which is their message, not their
own views on the needs of the day. Oscar Cullmann sees the
link with the apostles not in any apostolic succession but in
this word:

In the only New Testament text that explicitly speaks of
the relation of the apostles to the Church that follows
them—I refer to the already mentioned section of the
high-priestly prayer in John 17: 20—the further working
of the apostles is connected not with the succession principle
but rather with the *word of the apostles*: "those who believe
through their word".[3]

With this we should set some words of A. G. Hebert, "The

truth of the Faith depends on the truth of the story which
the Bible tells, of the working out in history of God's saving
purpose."[4]

All this has consequences for us. Just as it was possible for
the men of Timothy's day to come to know the sound words
of Jesus, so is it for us. The incarnate Son of God still comes
to his people in the faithful preaching of his word. Faith comes
by what is heard and "what is heard comes by the preaching
of Christ" (Rom. 10: 17). When faith comes Christ comes.
We are not concerned here with some abstruse doctrine, fit
only for the ivory towers and musty tomes of scholars. We
are concerned with a truth essential for vital religion. Over
and over it has been shown that there is a power of regenerating
faith and renewing life in the sound words of Scripture. "So
in the preaching of the gospel out of the pages of the New
Testament the modality of the incarnation as special revelation is continued; and when men believe this witness by
responding to it with saving faith, then Christ comes also to
the heart."[5]

The Four Gospels

The factuality of the message is emphasised by the use of the
Gospel form. It is generally agreed that this is unique to
Christianity. "To the Gospels as a whole there is no known
parallel or analogy."[6] There are distant parallels in the
biographies of some of the great ones of antiquity and in parts
of the Old Testament some have discerned vague likenesses
to the teaching of Jesus. But to the Gospels as a whole there
is no real parallel. The Evangelists have evolved a new
literary form to get their message across. Other forms were
available, for example the epistle, and the New Testament
bears ample testimony to the fact that the early Christians
were able to use the epistolary form with great effect. But
when they wrote about Jesus they used the Gospel form.
There may have been a number of reasons for this, but one
of them was surely that they wanted a form which found a
large place for the historical. They were concerned that the
facts of the life, death, resurrection and ascension of Jesus
become known. The historical is significant.

It is significant because above all Christianity calls for
faith in Jesus. It does not call simply for a life lived in con-
formity with certain precepts or principles. The Christian
life is undoubtedly important and in every age Christian

thinkers have put stress on the fact. But the very central thing is trust in a person and that person Jesus Christ. Now we cannot trust anyone we do not know. We may be optimistic about such a person. Indeed, on the recommendation of someone we know we may even be prepared to give some support to an unknown man's programme. But we cannot, we simply cannot trust a person we do not know. So when men are called on to put their trust in Jesus it is imperative that they be able to come to know him. Conceivably in the first days of the church men might have come to know him through the testimony of others who had seen and heard him. But for all later generations he is accessible only through the written record. "The only real Christ is the Christ presented in the Scriptures."[7] If we cannot trust the record we cannot know Jesus. And if we cannot know him it is idle nonsense to call on us to trust him.

Some scholars so emphasise the importance of the historical method they practise that in effect they rule out the possibility of knowing Jesus unless he conforms to the general human pattern. This may happen when analogy is stressed. Thus A. O. Dyson can say, "only by analogy with phenomena which occur in and around us can we recognise similar phenomena in historical material, and so attest their probability."[8] He goes on from this to the position that religious tradition can be understood only by analogy: "Religious tradition can only become comprehensible when it is seen in reciprocal connection with the whole religious and cultural history of mankind."[9] This rules out in advance any special occurrence such as the incarnation. Since we have no analogy for it we cannot recognise it.

But this is to make analogy too narrow a criterion. It fails to take notice of the fact that the Christian has always maintained that the incarnation is unique, that there are and can be no analogies. The fact that the Christian makes such a claim does not, of course, guarantee its truth. But it does mean that a flat statement that we can accept only what is supported by analogy is inadequate. It rules out the Christian position in advance. It is better instead to rely on evidence. If there is evidence that once God acted decisively in and for man then that evidence is to be accepted. It is not to be rejected on the grounds that we have no analogy for the unique.

Throughout the Bible there is a mixture of the human

and the divine. The purpose of God is there, but it is worked out through human agents. God's action is there and man's action is there. The techniques of the historian enable him to speak with authority about the human side of things. But historical techniques give no insight into the divine side. It is going beyond what is permissible to ask the historian to pronounce on such matters. As James D. Smart says, all that we can ask of the historian "is that he leave the door open to the credibility of divine action in history".[10] But this we can ask. The pity of it is that sometimes people impressed with what the techniques of the scientific historian can do go on to suggest that when the historian is through the whole story has been told. This the Christian cannot concede. His whole position depends on the fact that behind the human agents is God. And "a descriptive historical science", as Smart reminds us, "cannot penetrate beyond human actions, experiences, and ideas to reconstruct the actuality of a relation of God with man."[11]

There is nothing, then, in a proper understanding of the historical to disturb the conviction that God has spoken and has acted. We must be on our guard lest we lightly read supernatural significance into perfectly natural occurrences. But we must equally be on our guard against limiting the power of God by denying what he has said or done. Specifically we must recognise that he has acted to bring men salvation. That is fundamental to the Christian way.

When we discuss revelation it is important to be clear on this, for revelation must not be separated from redemption. The whole Bible is eloquent of God's tender concern for men and his will to save them from their sin. Revelation is never simply for the purpose of imparting interesting information. Every Christian must at times have felt exasperated because he could not find the answer to some problem in the Bible. But the Bible was never intended as a handbook of Christian doctrine, a compendium of Christian knowledge. It is the record of God's saving acts and it is given to man to enable him to enter that salvation. It is not exhaustive, but it is sufficient. It contains what man needs for salvation, even though it leaves much unexplained. We must be clear that revelation is not an end in itself. Christianity is not another variety of Gnosticism.

NOTES

1. Paul Althaus cited by Jacob A. O. Preus, *It is Written* (St. Louis: 1971), p. 57.
2. Carl F. H. Henry (ed.), *Revelation and the Bible* (London: 1959), p. 9.
3. Oscar Cullmann, *Peter, Disciple, Apostle, Martyr* (London: 1962), p. 226.
4. A. G. Hebert, *Scripture and the Faith* (New York: 1962), p. 60.
5. B. Ramm, *Special Revelation and the Word of God* (Grand Rapids: 1971), p. 116.
6. Harald Riesenfeld, *The Gospel Tradition* (Oxford: 1970), p. 2.
7. B. Ramm, *Special Revelation and the Word of God*, p. 116.
8. A. O. Dyson, *Who is Jesus Christ?* (London: 1969), p. 38.
9. *Ibid.*, p. 39 (this is an inference Troeltsch makes about theological method).
10. James D. Smart, *The Strange Silence of the Bible in the Church* (London: 1970), p. 110.
11. *Ibid.*, p. 115.

CHAPTER 8

The Authority of the Bible

IT FOLLOWS FROM the fact that the Bible records God's saving acts that it is a book which has authority. It is this book which points men to the way in which God would have them go. There is that which is divine about the Bible as well as that which is human. It is important that we recognise the place of the divine. When the preacher takes his Bible into the pulpit on Sunday morning he needs a word from God. He does not speak simply as an educated man who has given thought to the problems of the day and offers his congregation some suggestions as to how they should face those problems. He does, of course, speak as an educated man. And he does presumably have some ideas of his own (he is apt to make a pretty mess of preaching if he has not). But that is not the whole story. If there is no more to it than that he will be an unholy failure. He is not an expert on economics or history or politics or any one of a multitude of other departments of life which are apt to provide the problems his people face.

He is an expert in the gospel. Whatever light he may shed on other areas it is only this that gives him his qualification to preach. He is to set forth the gospel of Jesus Christ. He is to exhort men to accept the challenge it provides and live by their faith in the Son of God who died for them. To do this he must know where authentic Christianity is to be found and what he may safely say in the name of Christ. No more than an elementary acquaintance with the history of the Christian church is needed to know that men have sometimes put forward the strangest of ideas and labelled them "Christian". How does the preacher know that what he is saying has any more right to the name? He cannot preach with any conviction unless he has some authority behind his words. Some, it is true, hold that a preacher may have nothing more than his own ideas. Thus Nineham claims that he preaches in the spirit of Leonard Hodgson's formula, "This is how *I* see it; can *you* not see it like that as well?"[1] This is most unsatisfactory. With all respect, why should a congregation be expected to listen to nothing more than the preacher's impressions? Why should any Christian think that his opinions are worth being imposed on a congregation? Throughout the history of Christianity the Bible has been seen as giving preachers their authority and we need good reason before giving up the idea.

Inerrancy
It is authority that is important rather than inerrancy. The Bible does not appear ever to claim inerrancy for itself, at least in set terms, though evangelicals have usually thought that this or something like it is implied by what Scripture does say. When, for example, a passage is introduced with "Thus saith the Lord" it has seemed to them that the words that follow must be accepted. We cannot accuse God of making mistakes.

All the more is this the case in that the Bible puts a good deal of emphasis on truth. God never lies (Tit. 1 : 2). He is true though every man prove false (Rom. 3 : 4). Persistently God is said to be true (John 3 : 33, 7 : 28, 8 : 26; 1 Thess. 1 : 9; 1 John 5 : 20; Rev. 3 : 7, 6 : 10). He is "the God of truth" (Isa. 65 : 16, also Ps. 31 : 5, Hebrew). His judgments are true (Rom. 2 : 2; Rev. 16 : 7). Christ is the truth (John 14 : 6), is full of truth (John 1 : 14) and is true (Rev. 19 : 11). He is the true light (John 1 : 9), the true bread (John 6 : 32) and the true vine (John 15 : 1). He bears true witness (John 8 : 14) and is the true witness (Rev. 3 : 14). He speaks the truth from God (John 8 : 40). Truth is in him (Eph. 4 : 21) and his truth may be in men (2 Cor. 11 : 10). The Spirit is "the Spirit of truth" (John 14 : 17, 15 : 26, 16 : 13, cf. 1 John 5 : 7) and he guides men into truth (John 16 : 13). God's word is truth (John 17 : 17). Sometimes "the truth of God" comes pretty near to meaning the gospel (Rom. 3 : 7), as does "the word of truth" (Eph. 1 : 13; Col. 1 : 5; 2 Tim. 2 : 15; Jas. 1 : 18), and there are references to the truth of the gospel (Gal. 2 : 5, 14; Col. 1 : 5), "the truth of Christ" (2 Cor.

11 : 10) and "the way of truth" (2 Pet. 2 : 2). Truth must be known (1 Tim. 2 : 4, 4 : 3; 2 Tim. 3 : 7; Heb. 10 : 26; 1 John 2 : 21), believed (2 Thess. 2 : 12f.), obeyed (Gal. 5 : 7; 1 Pet. 1 : 22), and loved (2 Thess. 2 : 10). Christians are "of the truth" (1 John 3 : 19) and the church is "the pillar and bulwark of the truth" (1 Tim. 3 : 15).

Admittedly the question of truth is not a simple one and whole books have been written round it. But the Bible's massive insistence on it must not be overlooked. It is more than a little difficult to think that when the first Christian preachers went forth to preach what they understood to be the word of God that they held any doubt as to its veracity. And it is more than a little difficult to think that modern preachers can improve on them in this respect.

A consequence of this is that in a number of places where it is not easy to see how the statements of the Bible are to be harmonised with facts derived from other sources, evangelicals have spent a lot of time and effort (and sometimes ingenuity) in trying to show that the Bible is right after all. When a solution is not apparent they have often pointed out that difficulties are not confined to this area of Christian doctrine. The Trinity, for example, is not exactly easy nor are the incarnation, the atonement and other doctrines. But in each case the Christian has said in effect, "The facts are such that I must accept this doctrine even though I cannot answer all the questions it poses." We cannot solve all the problems posed by the doctrine of the Trinity. But neither would most Christians jettison it. The facts won't let them. So, it is urged, with revelation. We may not be able to explain just how the teaching of the Bible is to be related to the latest findings of science. But that does not mean that we surrender the teachings of the Bible. They have proved themselves over and over in the areas we can understand and we dare not abandon them in the places where we find difficulty.

There is a place for seeking out the meaning of difficult passages and relating it to our best ascertained knowledge from other sources. There is no future for a Christianity that is obscurantist. But the purpose of the Bible is not to give us information on scientific matters. Such truths are susceptible to discovery by our own efforts and God has left them to be found out in this way. They are not the proper subject of revelation. I do not mean that we can cheerfully accept all manner of scientific error and regard this as irrelevant. If the

Bible keeps making mistakes in matters scientific the suspicion arises that this flaw in the background is going to distort the foreground. But we should be clear on what the Bible writers were trying to do. And that was not write science for twentieth-century man. Karl Rahner reminds us that we must take care not to attribute to the sacred writers things they do not mean:

> It remains true that whatever the human writer intends to affirm as true according to his conviction and to which he required a real assent on our part, is also God's utterance and hence free from errors. Nevertheless, a consideration of the literary form, which is attributable to man alone, and not to God, may in many cases lead us to a more discreet, and possibly more restricted, estimate of what the sacred writer intended to affirm.[2]

We should notice further that there is progression in the Bible. Earlier revelation is filled out by later. We must not expect and we do not find the full revelation at the earlier time. But progression and development are not the same as error. Sometimes the concept of "progressive revelation" has been used as a means of discrediting some parts of the Bible which are regarded as "primitive". But unfortunately for this view the Bible does not show a steady progression from the lower to the higher, and upholders of the view have had to postulate not inconsiderable areas of deterioration as well as progression. In fact the idea could be held only by a selective choosing of incidents to demonstrate a progression and ignoring the rest. But even though we reject this concept it remains that the later revelation often builds upon and fills out the earlier. John Stott uses the illustration of the artist who makes a preliminary sketch and proceeds to fill in the canvas bit by bit.[3] The sketch is not the final shape. But it is adequate at the stage at which it is produced.

Geoffrey Bromiley points up a problem for those who dismiss inerrancy and yet seek to retain the idea that the Bible gives us the revelation of God's truth: "while it is no doubt a paradox that eternal truth is revealed in temporal events and witnessed through a human book, it is sheer unreason to say that truth is revealed in and through that which is erroneous."[4] It is this that makes the problem a serious one. If the Bible is basically astray, it is hard to see how we can trust it to give us God's truth.

An Authoritative Standard

It is important that we can trust it. Our primary concern is with its authority. Our solution to a particular difficulty may not be important but it is desperately important that we can go to the Bible with a firm trust in it. Unless we can receive it as God's authoritative word we are back on our own resources. Our energies are better employed in showing that the Bible is authoritative than in contending for our solutions of difficult problems.

This is a legitimate procedure, for the fact is that nobody comes to regard the Bible as the book that gives us God's word because he has worked through it and come up with acceptable solutions to all the difficulties. He accepts it thankfully and regards it as reliable because that was the view of Christ and his apostles. It is this, and not our ability to explain difficulties, that is the justification for our holding the Bible to be God's authoritative revelation. Conversely our inability to come up with satisfactory explanations does not compel us to abandon the Bible.

I have spoken of the value the Bible has for the preacher as the authority to which he can appeal as he exhorts men to follow the way of God. But it has value also for the man in the pew. From time to time men rise up in the church with new and unusual teachings. How are we to know whether they are departing from authentic Christianity or bringing us new and important implications of the faith? There must be some standard to which we can appeal.

For that matter the church needs such a standard for her day to day life. From time to time the church is called upon to say something about the problems arising from the community in which she is set. There may be a demand for an official statement or her members may be required to speak for themselves. In either case more than a private opinion is needed if the Christian position is sought. There must be some standard by which the Christian position can be determined. Again we come back to the need for a final authority.

This does not mean that either the preacher or the church clamours for an authority and after a hunt for something suitable comes up with the Bible. No. Rather, the Bible has always been the authority for Christians. The church never existed without a Bible to turn to. It is in the nature of things that from time to time an authority of some sort is required. And for Christians that authority is not one arbitrarily chosen. It is the Bible in which Christians have always seen their authority to rest. It is the Bible against which Christians measure their beliefs and practices. It is there that they find what Christianity was and is and it is there accordingly that they can find whether they are in the genuine succession of authentic Christianity or whether they have gone grievously astray.

Part of our problem, of course, consists in today's widespread rejection of authority. It is not that Christians, while retaining respect for all other sorts of authority, have suddenly found themselves calling in question the authority of the Bible. The problem is that we live in an age which is calling in question authority in all its forms. The young are questioning the authority of the old, and especially that of their parents. The authority of the State (particularly the State in which we happen to live) is doubted. So is that of all the traditional "authority figures" whether in church or community. It would be surprising if in this ferment the authority of the Bible were not called in question by some. But we should be clear that the questioning is more a part of the spirit of our age than a new demand arising from closer attention to the essential nature of the Christian faith. When we undertake that close scrutiny we find that the reasons for thinking of the Bible as authoritative are just as valid as ever they were. Those reasons may not be accepted by some of our revolting generation. But that does not make them invalid.

It is worth pointing out that even the most anarchical among us must, in the last resort, pay attention to his ultimate authority. This may be nothing more exciting than himself or his peers. Or it may be a society or a State or an ideal he has picked up somewhere. I do not mean that a man will necessarily say to himself, "I must make a decision. I will now appeal to my ultimate authority." But when he has a far-reaching decision to make he will necessarily make it with reference to what he holds most dear. If he professes to be a Christian he may reject the Bible as his authority, but that does not mean that he rejects authority. When he makes his decision whether the course before him is compatible with the Christian faith or not his real view about ultimate authority comes into play. He may make his decision because this is the way the revolutionary group to which he belongs would act (or because he thinks it would). He may choose the course that the institution stands for or the course that the institution does not stand for. He may simply choose that which appeals to himself personally in which case he makes himself his ultimate authority. But unless he is acting capriciously he is acting in response to what he sees as finally authoritative.

In the whole history of Christianity it seems that believers have been able to come up with no more than three ideas about the ultimate authority. Some see it in the Bible, some in the church (or a group within the church or outside it; the essence of this view is corporateness), and others in something personal, be it the reason or spiritual experience. Of course in practice we all give some attention to all three. But in the last resort we all see one or other as what really matters. The popularity of the personal today ought not to blind us to the fact that there are still good reasons for holding to the classic view of Christians, that the Bible is God's authoritative word.

And for all its popularity, the view that what matters ultimately is what appeals to the individual's experience or reason is a profoundly pessimistic view. It means that we have nothing from which to correct our errors, no way of knowing what is true or false once we have accepted an idea. If man's mind is the measure of things there is no way of getting back to the right way once that mind has gone off on the wrong track. Only the most pessimistic among us can be comfortable with such a view.

Cultural Relativity

Objection is sometimes made these days to the reliability of the Bible, with whatever consequences this entails for us, on the ground that there are considerable differences between one part of the Bible and another and between all the parts and the views of men of our own day. The cultural relativity of all man's literary activities, it is contended, makes it impossible for us to take the Bible seriously. It is urged that any literary work has its meaning only in terms of the culture in which it was produced. Men of another day may indeed contemplate it, but they will certainly get it wrong because their own culture is different. They cannot help reading some of their own background into what they are reading. There is no way in which a man can cut himself off from his own cultural environment.

So when any of the Bible writers is writing of events or teaching of a time or a culture other than his own he will misinterpret those events or teachings precisely because his own culture is different. And we in the twentieth century repeat the process. We appear to be left with our cultural misinterpretations of the writer's cultural misinterpretations. And always, we are told, we must have in the back of our minds the thought that if we had been there and seen and heard what the Bible writer is reporting we would probably have expressed it differently. Where the Bible writer saw a miracle, for example, we ask whether we, with our very different background, would have felt that a supernatural explanation was called for had we been there.

A partial answer to this is that it represents no more than our own cultural reaction, a reaction moreover which commonly assumes that our culture is superior to other cultures. We must be on our guard against the unspoken assumption that we have a superior standpoint so that others must be adjudged inferior in comparison to us. Nothing that is merely a cultural expression of our own day can be held to have permanent validity. The argument is self-defeating.

Yet something remains. The argument does not necessarily demand that our culture be superior, only that it be different. If that is the way of it, then the whole question of cultural transfer arises.

It is therefore a more telling rebuttal to point out that no man need be marooned on the island of his own culture to such an extent that he cannot appreciate what men in other cultures are saying to him. Granted that we can never get out of our own skins, it remains that cultures are not necessarily mutually incomprehensible. We must always exercise care when we interpret works from men of other cultures and it will require restraint lest we make the mistake of thinking that they mean exactly what we would mean. But it would be nonsense to say that we cannot understand them. That would mean that we all manifest a certain passivity, that we are all tangled in our own traditional patterns to such a degree that we cannot understand anything outside. But all creative thinking, all sympathetic putting of ourselves in the place of others cries out against the idea. If we must not overlook the force of cultural relativism we must not exaggerate it either. Especially is this the case when, as with the Bible, there is a continuous history, an unbroken connection with those who wrote the book. From generation to generation the cultural gap has been spanned and we receive the Bible, not as something that descends on us from outer space, but as part of our own culture. There is continuity as well as discontinuity.

James Barr tells us that his friends who espouse the cultural relativist position "are commonly people of some considerable independence of mind, of radicalism and nonconformity — a fact which both does them credit as persons and does damage to the force of their own argument."[5] He finds a further argument against that position in that it is possible for literary appreciation to take place, even of works from another culture than our own. Such literary appreciation is the constant task of the literary critic. Homer, to take an example, is not meaningless to the modern student. Any competent critic can make something of this author (or authors). It would be nonsense to suggest that because our culture is so very different from that of the author we cannot study the writing. We can and do. As Barr says, "The argument for cultural relativism, in fact, is deeply in contradiction with the appeal to literary appreciation."[6]

A position somewhat akin to this is that which sees the traditional attitude to the Bible as stemming from a world view that we can no longer accept. To the man of old, it is said, this whole world is God's world and God may be expected to intervene at any time. Even what we call the world of nature was subject to unpredictable divine intervention and this was, of course, much more the case in the affairs of men. The activity of spirits, angels and devils was taken as a matter of course. How else could phenomena be explained?

To men with a scientific background all this is nonsense. The scientist sees all that happens in nature as explicable along the lines of natural laws, at least in principle. Certainly he sees no reason for invoking the supernatural as the explanation of the phenomena he studies. And the positions of the psychologist and the sociologist as they study human life are not essentially dissimilar.

The result is that we live out our lives in a framework different from that of the men of the Bible. We no longer expect that the causes they took for granted will operate. It is inferred that we can no longer accept the Bible with its record of "the mighty works of God".

To this a number of things should be said. One is that the inference is wrongly drawn. When the men of the Bible spoke of God as acting they were not drawing attention to a commonplace. They were speaking of what was unique. It may well be that they were more ready than we to see the miraculous but that does not mean that when they spoke of the mighty acts of God they were simply using the language of everyday life. It is not sufficiently appreciated that the men of the Bible were sparing in their view of the miraculous. They saw a cluster of miracles at the time of the exodus, associated with the emergence of the people of God. They saw another in the days of Elijah and Elisha when prophecy began. And there is a third group at the coming of Jesus and lasting on until the first days of the church. Apart from these three, for which a special reason can be assigned in each case, miracles are rare. The Bible records passages of hundreds of years without mentioning miracle. We should not exaggerate the extent of the miraculous in Scripture.

Again it should not be assumed, as it too often is, that men of Bible days could not handle language as we can. With us there is no problem in the use of spatial metaphors, as when we speak of "the top man", "the corners of the earth", "the rat race" and much more. Nobody will accuse us of thinking of a literal pyramid with one man at the summit or of the earth as rectangular, or of rats as running in a literal race when we use such terms. It is sheer arrogance when we insist that the ancients could not manage this feat. It is natural to use the metaphor of height to refer to what is good or great; and it is moving too fast when we take every reference to God as highly exalted in an ancient author to mean that God lives in a home vertically above the earth. That view may have been held. I am not denying it. But I am denying that every statement in the Bible about heaven is to be taken with full literalness. Even today we sometimes hear people sing

There's a Friend for little children
Above the bright blue sky.

But that does not mean that the people who sing the hymn envisage a heaven vertically above them. The metaphor is obvious and we use it without hesitation. We ought to bear in mind the possibility that the men of the Bible could do the same.

In this age of secular theology it should not be necessary to demonstrate that God is in all of life. And if he is, then the biblical readiness to see his hand everywhere is quite natural. We cannot separate the sacred from the secular. We cannot hand over whole areas of life to the scientist, the psychologist and the sociologist and confine God to the narrowly "spiritual". If the Bible writer speaks of an action of God in history we may perhaps think that we would not have expressed it in quite the same way; but unless we are prepared to deny that God is in all his creation we cannot rule out the possibility that God has in fact acted.

It is further to be noted that there can usually be more than one explanation of things. The scientific explanation, while complete in itself, is not the only explanation of phenomena. It is quite possible, for example, to give in principle a complete explanation of the workings of a computer in terms of electronics and the like. But this does not dispose of the fact that a complete explanation can also be given in terms of the purpose of the programmer. Neither makes the other wrong and each may be complete in itself. So with the Bible. It is too easy to say, "The ancients saw God in everything, but our scientific explanation does away with the need of that hypothesis." That science has the answers to a lot of questions does not make the Bible irrelevant. For the fact is that our scientific explanation is always an answer to the question, "How?" It explains how things work the way they do. But it does not deal in ultimate questions. It does not answer the question, "Why?" For that, the explanation in terms of ultimate purpose, the biblical answer, is still needed. When the modern man opts for his scientific explanation and looks no further he is begging the question. For God is not the end result of any scientific experiment or observation.

There are, then, many assaults on the traditional view of the Bible and its authority. I certainly do not take up the position that these can be neglected or that the orthodox cannot learn from them. It seems clear that some traditional positions must be looked at carefully in the light of modern criticisms.

But on the basic point, that we can still regard the Bible as reliable and use it as our authoritative standard, I see no reason for abandoning the traditional position. There is good reason for holding that God has spoken in Scripture and where God speaks it is the part of man to hear and obey.

NOTES

1. D. E. Nineham, *Bulletin of the John Rylands Library*, Vol. 52 (1969–70), p. 193.
2. Karl Rahner, *Inspiration in the Bible* (London: 1964), p. 83.
3. John Stott, *Understanding the Bible* (Sydney: 1972), p. 160.
4. F. Davidson, A. M. Stibbs, and E. F. Kevan (eds.), *The New Bible Commentary* (London: 1954), p. 22.
5. James Barr, *The Bible in the Modern World* (London: 1973), p. 47.
6. *Ibid.*, p. 73.

CHAPTER 9

Revelation Outside Christianity

CONTEMPORARY CHRISTIAN SCHOLARS are much more ready to see genuine revelation in the great non-Christian religions than were their forbears. They understand revelation not as so many propositions but as encounters with God. Isaiah and Jeremiah and Paul had such encounters and the record is in the Bible. But, they ask, may there not have been other encounters? May not the Buddha have really met God? Or Muhammed? May not the Scriptures of Buddhism and of Islam give us revelation that is just as real as that in the Bible?

They often respond with unhesitating affirmatives. There is no denying the reality of the experience of some, at any rate, of the saints in all the great religions of the world and if experience is to be the criterion, then these religions have revelation just as real as that of Christianity. Many modern students of these religions contend that Christians should not try to evangelise (the word often used is "proselytise") their adherents. It is better, they say, for dialogue to take place. So they suggest that Christians sit down and talk with Hindus and the rest. All may conceivably learn from the others. Those who hold such views censure "spiritual imperialism" as they criticise the traditional work of missions.

Ninian Smart proposes explicitly that, when we examine the religions of the world, experience be our test for truth. After some discussion of the ideas put forward by a number of religions he says, "In brief, then, one test of truth which I propose is this—that a system of revealed truth or doctrine should reflect the experience of great men in particular and of all religious men in a general way."[1] He agrees that this is undemocratic, but "it seems absurd to treat the lives of ordinary folk as on a par, in this context, with those of St. John of the Cross, the Buddha and so on."[2] He is clear that it is experience that is the criterion.

In an earlier chapter I objected to ways of understanding revelation that concentrate on subjective religious experiences. Such objections apply here also. Smart sees no reason why we should put St. John of the Cross or the Buddha on a par with ordinary folk. Maybe we should not, but it is worth asking, "Why not?" As far as I can see Smart lacks any criterion for deciding between them. He prefers his elite, but I do not see on what grounds he could object to someone who made a different choice.

Experience is scarcely a sufficient criterion. But if we reject it, and accept instead the revelation in the Bible, that does not dispose of the question. A. G. Hebert makes the point that "God's choice of Israel to be His own people does not mean that God had no care for the other nations of mankind, such as the Greeks and Romans, the Indians and the Chinese. On the contrary, it is emphasised from the start that God is the creator of the world and of all men. God had things to teach the other nations also."[3] It is biblical teaching that God "did not leave himself without witness" among the heathen (Acts 14: 17). The centurion Cornelius's prayers and alms "have ascended as a memorial before God" (Acts 10: 4) and Peter, after his contact with this man could say, "Truly I perceive that God shows no partiality, but in every nation any one who fears him and does what is right is acceptable to him" (Acts 10: 35). Paul accepted the testimony of some of the Greek poets as giving certain truths about God (Acts 17: 28). He writes to the Romans, "what can be known about God is plain to them (i.e. the Gentiles), because God has shown it to them" (Rom. 1: 19). He also said, "When Gentiles who have not the law do by nature what the law requires, they are a law unto themselves, even though they do not have the law. They show that what the law requires is written on their hearts, while their conscience also bears witness" (Rom. 2: 14f.).

It is plain that the New Testament writers saw God as active in the nations at large as well as in Israel, his own people. This is to be understood not only as an activity concerned with such matters as rewarding good actions and punishing evil ones, but also as giving revelation in some measure. The

extent of this revelation may be debatable, but as to the fact
of it there should surely be no doubt.

Unfortunately the Bible gives no criterion whereby we can
tell what is really revelation outside it. It lets us know that
there is such a thing, but not much more. And there is nothing
to encourage the idea that any revelation outside the Bible
is to be regarded as having the same definitive function as
the Bible. Jesus constantly appeals to Scripture to establish
doctrine and so do his apostles. But there is nothing to show
that Christian doctrine can be established on the basis of any
revelation made among the nations at large.

Here I think everything hangs on the age old question,
"What think ye of Christ?" If he is really the only begotten
Son of God then it is manifest that no one can be ranked with
him. It follows that his teaching must be the standard and the
only teaching to be accepted is that which agrees with his.
If we reject the uniqueness of Christ then there seems no
standard and we may well regard all "revelations" as on
much the same level.

We should be clear that it is the Christ and not "the
Christian religion" for which finality is claimed. Christians
have all too often obscured the revelation with their ecclesiastical trappings and have offered men a form of piety instead
of the gospel. Lesslie Newbigin speaks of

> the announcement of an event which concerns the whole
> human situation and not merely one aspect of it—the
> religious aspect, for example. It is the announcement of
> the reign of God present and active. It sends Jesus and his
> disciples out on a mission which includes healing the sick
> and feeding the hungry as well as preaching the good news
> and teaching the way of life. But it does not lead to the
> creation of a theocratic welfare state in Israel; it leads to
> rejection, crucifixion and death. And yet death is not the
> end; beyond death is resurrection and the coming of the
> new era of the Spirit—promise and guarantee of a new
> creation, of new heavens and a new earth, of the new
> Jerusalem.[4]

It is this understanding of the Christian way which enables
him to speak of what we are offered in Christ in these terms:
"We are not offered something which might be described as
the best among the religions; we are offered something which,

if it is true, is the clue to all history — the history of the world, and the history of my own soul."[5]

All this breathes the convictions that it is no less than God who has acted in Christ and that the action he has taken is decisive. It is this and not some supposed superiority of Christians to members of other religions that is to be stressed. In the light of the cross the Christian has nothing of which to boast. He sees himself as a sinner, deserving of nothing but condemnation. But he sees also that God has acted in grace to bring men salvation. And, since the record of what God has done is in the Bible, this gives a special place to the Bible. Apart from it how are men to know what God has done for them?

Isolation is Past

Christianity built up its theology largely in isolation from other religions and certainly with no significant reference to faiths like Buddhism. In the sure conviction that God has spoken Christians went ahead to erect their doctrinal systems without taking seriously the possibility that there might have been some revelations on which these other faiths are based. Now that we know more about such religions, and indeed must live in the kind of contact with them that was not dreamed of in earlier days, it is urged that we take another look at the situation. We may well find that the Christian claim should now be toned down and the revelations underlying other religions be taken just as seriously as the Christian revelation.

There is place and need for a proper humility here. As I have already argued, we need deny none of God's good gifts made outside Christianity. But that does not mean that we should deny any of his good gifts within the Christian sphere. If Jesus Christ was the unique Son of God, then that remains, whatever truths may be in the possession of Islam and the rest. If God has spoken through the prophets then nothing that he has said to other men renders that null and void. If Christians through the centuries have relied trustfully on the revelation and found the deep needs of their souls satisfied then that still stands. We must not ask Christians to renounce their well-proven convictions on the ground that God has not left himself without witness elsewhere.

It is sometimes argued that the situation is a little like that in our understanding of natural science. In the Ptolemaic system men held firmly to the view that the earth was the centre of the universe. But the fact that many men, generation after generation, held the view did not make it right. In the light of the fuller revelation made available in modern times, thinking men simply had to abandon the Ptolemaic conception. There was no other possibility. So, it is said, in the area of religion. At one time many men believed that there was only one revelation of God and they evolved their systems accordingly. Now that it is clear that others than Christians know something of God the Christian claim must be abandoned.

But this is to go too far, too fast. Our new knowledge of the other great religions of the world does not invalidate anything in the Christian faith. The two positions are not strictly comparable at all. The Ptolemaic astronomy or any other astronomy was and is held by the mass of men, not because they have any real knowledge of it or committal to it, but simply because it is what the experts say. Men in general have little means of checking. They accept the word of the experts.

But Christianity is another thing again. It is true that there are some areas in which we are dependent on the experts (the meaning of the Greek terms in which the New Testament is written, for example). But it is also true that Christianity is not simply an assortment of facts on the scientific model. It is a way of life. It is an invitation to repent and believe in Christ and to walk trustfully with God. Personal experience and personal commitment are of the very essence.

It is true that modern Christians have knowledge about other faiths that their forbears lacked. It is true that some Christian formulations might have been better made had it been possible to take notice of what other theists claim. It is true that there is no room for spiritual arrogance. But it is also true that nothing in our knowledge of the ways other men approach God compels us to deny the truth of the Christian revelation or to renounce centuries of Christian experience. It is still as true as ever it was that whoever comes to Christ finds rest for his soul (Matt. 11 : 28ff.). Some claims for Christian uniqueness most go. But that does not affect the heart of the matter. It does not affect the truth that God has spoken and that what he has said is still relevant to the needs of men. Bishop Chandu Ray can register an objection to the method of a congress on evangelism which concentrated on the "irreligious" world. "Little or no attention was given to grappling with the two thousand million people of the *religious* *world* who are mostly in Asia—those who have a deeply rooted faith in God through their own religion and need to know where and how the revelation of God in Jesus Christ meets their knowledge and faith."[6] Bishop Ray does not deny the reality of the faith in God brought about by the religions of Asia. But he recognises that the reality of this faith is no reason for minimising the importance of God's revelation in Christ or the *need* of Asia for that revelation. The judgment of this distinguished Asian, familiar with the religions of Asia from his birth, should not lightly be neglected.

Exclusiveness
One modern emphasis says that Christians must not take up an exclusive position. The advance of modern knowledge shows that there is much truth in all the nations of the world. Any nation or religion that claims exclusive prerogatives shows itself unreliable by that very fact. James D. Smart puts it this way:

> The exploration of cultures and religions other than our own has shown a fair measure of wisdom distributed among all of them. No nation has had truth or goodness for its private preserve. Therefore an Israel that claims an exclusive role as witness to the one true God or a Christian church that regards itself as the sole repository and guarantee of divine truth seems to exhibit a narrowness of mind that is no longer tolerable.[7]

Nobody wants to convict himself of narrowness of mind, so the point is taken as proved.

But it is not so simple. It is not a question of whether we want to be thought broad or narrow minded. It is not a question either of denying the good gifts that God has given to others. It is a question of truth. If it is true that "in Christ God was reconciling the world to himself" (2 Cor. 5: 19), then it is no service to anyone to deny the fact in the interest of broadmindedness. It is the truth with which we must be concerned however unpopular that may be.

And the truth is that Christianity is concerned ineluctably with the particular. At the heart of the faith there is a cross and without that cross and all it means Christianity would not be Christianity. Ramm brings out the significance of this for our understanding of revelation:

> The death of Christ by crucifixion was one death among tens of thousands, and in itself bore no marks of any transcendent significance. But what is it which makes *this* the center of Christian faith and piety? What elevates *this* cross above the painful crosses of countless other victims? What gives *this* cross its great significance to the human race? *It is the inner thought of God about the cross, spoken out in language by virtue of special revelation which raises the cross of Christ above all other crosses and reveals it as the event of world redemption.*[8]

We must make up our minds whether we are going to accept Christianity's central affirmation. Unless we believe that God acted decisively in Christ for man's salvation it is hard to see what claim we have on the name "Christian". But if we do, we must affirm that there was something about Christ's cross that sets it apart from all the other crosses of antiquity, something about his suffering that makes it different from the world's agony through the ages. Once we admit its difference we must accord to the record on which we depend for our information about it a difference from other literature. This is not to deny whatever good gifts God has given to the men of other religions. We must thankfully acknowledge them. But that does not imply that we cease to thank him for the unique event in Christ.

The uniqueness of Christ is part of Christianity. There is a difference between the way the prophets and apostles spoke and the way Jesus spoke. Their authority was derivative, his native. They pointed to him, but he spoke with the very authority of God. In this he differs from the founders of the world's religions. As Ramm puts it:

> Christ is no seeker, no religious experimenter, no religious pilgrim searching for the higher path. Nor is he the determined mystic who will not rest until he has united with God. On the contrary, he is the *Logos* in full possession of the truth. He is the *Light* which shines into this dark world. He is the Prophet who speaks with perfect clarity the word of God. He is the *Teacher* whose mastery of his subject is perfect. He is the *Son* who is in the ideal position to disclose the mind of his Father.[9]

This uniqueness is sometimes roundly denied. A. O. Dyson cites Jaspers, "No man can be God; God speaks exclusively through no man, and what is more, his speech through every man has many meanings."[10] Dyson goes on to speak approvingly of "the freeing of Christian theology from the claim to exclusivity".[11] He also summarises the position of Schubert Ogden in these terms:

> we cannot postulate only one event in which the turning of that loving God is uniquely and exclusively located. When God is understood in this way, we have to allow that every man in every place and at every time has to be seen as a "man-who-comes-from-God" and as a "man-to-whom-God-is-turned". This means that, in whatever way we are to understand Jesus Christ, we cannot understand him as contradicting this insight.[12]

We could scarcely have a more universalistic view than this. Nor one that is at one and the same time more contradictory of the evidence mankind affords us and neglectful of that in Scripture. It is true that every man is the object of God's love, but it does not follow that every man is equally with every other man a source of knowledge about God. The most elementary acquaintance with our species is evidence for that. And this view overlooks what we learn from Scripture about God. It is plain that, *pace* Ogden, Jesus was different from "every man in every place and at every time". In our democratic age we may not like this. But facts are facts.

Or we might think of Fritz Buri, another who strongly opposes any Christian claim to exclusiveness. "Even the New Testament record does not restrict the locus of the Christ merely to Jesus but suggests a much wider dominion." And again, "this event occurs wherever man understands himself as absolutely responsible and experiences the fulfilment of his destiny. . . . Certainly this viewpoint is not limited to Jesus Christ and the realm of symbols and sensibility connected to his name."[13] Again we have the language of dogmatic assertion. And again there is no reckoning with the way the Bible pictures Jesus. But there is no other way than through the Bible of getting at the evidence about Jesus.

Some scholars are reminding us that it is important in this connection to pay careful attention to the meaning of the words we use. Thus Gordon D. Kaufman discusses the view that we need not accept the Old Testament view that Yahweh has performed the "mighty acts" it narrates. He points out that this is to neglect "the significance of the fact that 'God' is a proper name, not a general term".[14] We are not to apply the English word "God" to any so-called deity. It gets its meaning precisely from what the Old Testament tells us of Yahweh. Without that complex of meaning we are misusing the term. This does not mean that God has been at work only in Israel. There is no reason to deny that he has been active in other cultures or that much may be learned from other religions. "But the point is that for those who use the word God such activity will be attributed to *him* — and not to 'Vishnu' or to 'Zeus'; and the word will be understood in terms derived from the (Hebraic-Western) history which created and formed it and gave it such meaning as it in fact has."[15]

The important point Kaufman makes with regard to the activity of God in other cultures and religions he puts in these terms:

> One can, if one wishes, relate that meaning to others derived from other cultural contexts — and every believer will surely want to hold that God has been active in all human cultures, not only the West — but this will involve attaching new predicates to the subject which the word God names; it will not be an exchange of that subject for another.[16]

It is some such attitude as this which we must adopt. No one wants to deny that God has been active throughout the world and throughout the centuries. But it is true to the Bible, and, as Kaufman insists, it is true to the linguistics of the case, that it is one God and one God only who has been active. That God is the God who reveals himself in the Old Testament (and the New). God may well have been active in many lands and at many times, but it is in the Bible that men have come to know him for what he is, to know him as God.

John V. Taylor stresses the point that Christ stands in judgment over all the world's religions, the "Christian religion" as well as the rest:

> It is not so much that he is the culmination or crown of every religion — that is not how I would express it — but

that in him each religion will be brought to fulfilment in terms true to itself, through crisis and conversion.[17]

This is not a denial of the real revelation in the various religions. Taylor thinks of a religion "as a people's tradition of response to the reality the Holy Spirit has set before their eyes."[18] We can accept this without implying that there is no difference in the revelation to which response is made. Moreover, in each religion on this view there is God's revelation indeed, but there is also the response people have made to that revelation, and Taylor sees this as just as true of the Christian religion as any other. The Christ always stands in judgment on religion.

I have been arguing that there is a finality about the revelation God has made in Christ. This does not carry with it the corollary that Christians have always made the kind of response to that revelation that they should. Too often we who name the name of Christ have been guilty of half-heartedness where the gospel calls for total commitment. We have been preoccupied with our comfortable ecclesiastical problems while we have ignored the world's agony. We have failed to bear in mind that the cross is at the heart of our faith and that the cross pronounces an annihilating judgment on all self-seeking. We have said happily enough, "We are the people" and have watered down the demand that we be crucified with Christ. We have been warned that judgment begins with the household of God (1 Pet. 4: 17). We should take heed to the warning.

In thinking of the way judgment hangs over all religion it is instructive to reflect on the attitude of the Jews to Jesus. No people had been as well prepared to understand the kingdom of God, the Messiah, the Suffering Servant, and so on. But when the Son of God came, they crucified him. They rejected the revelation. It is a fallacy to think that all religions amount to much the same, so that all that is necessary is for a man to follow the religion in which he was born. It is possible for men in any religion to reject the revelation in their zeal for religiosity. Christians must not see themselves as immune to the temptation.

Perhaps we should notice another point made by Taylor, namely that Christ is Lord of every man and meets every man's need. He points to the kind of dialogue that can take place wherein the Christian listens only so that he can await his turn to speak and press the claims of his Saviour. But the Christian may also listen until he sees something "of that other man's real world". Taylor says, "I shall see past what to me are distasteful rituals, alien symbols and concepts that carry no conviction to the insights they are trying to express." He lists other things and concludes,

> as a final bestowal, I shall be given access to the dark places of that stranger's world—the things that really make him ashamed or anxious or despairing. And then at last, I shall see the Saviour and Lord of *that* world, my Lord Jesus, and yet not as I have known him. I shall understand how perfectly he matches all the needs and all the aspirations and all the insights of that other world—He who is the unique Lord and Saviour of all possible worlds.[19]

Here there is the recognition of the very real truths by which that other man lives. But that recognition does not prevent Taylor from seeing the special place that belongs to Jesus and to the revelation he brings.

For our present purpose the important thing is to notice that it is the Christ revealed in Scripture who is thus finally authoritative for all men. Christians must constantly reform their thinking and their practice by reference to that Christ. But neither their need of reform nor their recognition that God has been active in the other religions of the world alters the fact that Christ is still the standard. "In Christ God was reconciling the world to himself" (2 Cor. 5: 19). It is still necessary to proclaim that Christ to the ends of the world and to bring men to know the revelation he has made.

NOTES

1. A. R. Vidler (ed.), *Soundings* (Cambridge: 1962), p. 116.
2. *Ibid.*
3. A. G. Hebert, *Scripture and the Faith* (New York: 1962), p. 56.
4. Lesslie Newbigin, *The Finality of Christ* (London: 1969), pp. 48f.
5. *Ibid.*, p. 62.
6. Bishop Chandu Ray, *Newsletter*, Vol. 6, no. 8, p. 2.
7. James D. Smart, *The Strange Silence of the Bible in the Church* (London: 1970), pp. 92f.
8. B. Ramm, *Special Revelation and the Word of God* (Grand Rapids: 1971), pp. 133f. (Ramm's italics).

9. *Ibid.*, p. 111 (Ramm's italics).
10. A. O. Dyson, *Who Is Jesus Christ?* (London: 1969), p. 81.
11. *Ibid.*, p. 82.
12. *Ibid.*, p. 67.
13. *Ibid.*, pp. 104f.
14. Gordon D. Kaufman, *Interpretation*, Vol. xxv (1971), p. 102.
15. *Ibid.*
16. *Ibid.*
17. John V. Taylor, *The Go-Between God* (London: 1973), p. 190.
18. *Ibid.*, p. 182.
19. *Ibid*, p. 189.